RECIPROCITY AND REDISTRIBUTION IN ANDEAN CIVILIZATIONS

Hau
BOOKS

www.haubooks.com

RECIPROCITY AND REDISTRIBUTION IN ANDEAN CIVILIZATIONS

John V. Murra

Transcript of the Lewis Henry Morgan Lectures
at the University of Rochester

April 8th – 17th, 1969

With annotations by
Freda Yancy Wolf and Heather Lechtman

Hau Books
Chicago

Cover and layout design: Sheehan Moore

Typesetting: Prepress Plus (www.prepressplus.in)

ISBN: 978-0-9973675-5-3
LCCN: 2017944264

Hau Books
Chicago Distribution Center
11030 S. Langley
Chicago, IL 60628
www.haubooks.com

Hau Books is marketed and distributed by The University of Chicago Press
www.press.uchicago.edu

Printed in the United States of America on acid-free paper.

Table of Contents

Foreword

The Lewis Henry Morgan lectures at the University of Rochester were inaugurated in 1962 and have been presented annually ever since. The lectures commemorate Morgan's contributions to the University of Rochester, his support for the founding of a women's college, and his legacy in anthropology, as reflected in the topics of the first three lectures, which focused on kinship (Meyer Fortes in 1963), native North Americans (Fred Eggan in 1964), and social evolution (Robert M. Adams in 1965).

As the oldest and longest-running anthropology lecture series in North America, the Morgan Lectures have produced some of the most influential texts in modern anthropology, to name but a few: Victor Turner's *The Ritual Process: Structure and Anti-structure* (1966), Marilyn Strathern's *After Nature: Kinship in the Late Twentieth Century* (1992), and Nancy Munn's *The Fame of Gawa: A Symbolic Study of Value Transformation in a Massim Society (Papua New Guinea)* (1986). A view of the lectures after more than fifty years illustrates the ways that anthropologists have moved well beyond Morgan's Enlightenment roots, and also how they have expanded upon the topics that preoccupied him: kinship and social organization, political economy, indigenous peoples, and cross-cultural comparison.

Many of the lectures have culminated in the publication of an original monograph. Some of them that have not appeared in print now enjoy a second life online, thanks to HAU, which has brought unpublished lectures from the past to a wider audience. The present volume is based on four lectures delivered by John Murra in Rochester in 1969, made available for the first time through the dedication of Heather Lechtman and the late Freda Wolf, with the generous support of the HAU editorial team. Lechtman and Wolf assembled the text of the lectures from incomplete typed transcriptions, as well as tapes of the lectures provided by the National Anthropological Archives of the Smithsonian Institution.

In these lectures, Murra presents a spirited, lucid, and erudite analysis of the development of Andean civilization, describing the forms of social, economic, and political organization that enabled large, dense populations to thrive at extremely high altitudes across vast distances. In doing so, Murra argues that the Andean model of sociopolitical development offers a challenge to the schema of social evolution first proposed by Morgan in *Ancient Society* and later taken up by Marx and Engels.

Murra's account demonstrates how archeology, archival research, and ethnography can be integrated to explore questions that shaped anthropology during Lewis Henry Morgan's lifetime and still remain central to our field today: Why and how did states develop? How did the colonial encounter transform precolonial social institutions? How does technological progress lead to new forms of political organization?

Murra ultimately concludes that the systems of reciprocity and redistribution that shaped Andean society led to the emergence of a vastly different kind of state than that which had been imagined by Morgan, Marx, or Engels. He argues that the Inka empire did not rely on large-scale slavery or feudal bonds, and managed to exert political and economic control through long term relationships of dependency that were not enforced "through the whip" (this volume, page 71). Though oriented to the past, his analysis leads us to ponder the future of economic and political organization in an era of rapid technological change. We now know that there were indeed many paths to "civilization." Where those paths may lead remains an open question.

Daniel R. Reichman
Robert J. Foster
Co-Directors, Lewis Henry Morgan Lecture Series
Department of Anthropology
University of Rochester
May 2017

The Andean "Avenue Towards Civilization"

John Murra's opening remarks in his first Morgan Lecture are a broadside; not a harsh attack, but a firm, insistent reckoning of Andean America as one among those regions in which pristine civilizations developed. He reiterated that data documenting the Andean achievement come not only from archaeology and ethnohistory, but from deeply pervasive continuities, as in the utilization of vertical ecologies, in agricultural technologies, in land tenure systems, in cloth production, that ethnographic studies establish as persistent among Andean communities, even to the present.

Murra recalls throughout the lectures the goal he pursued in structuring them.

> From Lecture 2, on reciprocity: "[…] I suggested that we might usefully look at some recent research in the Andes, at the few moments in the Andean continuum that have emerged in just the last few years, and which might shed some light on the general problem of achieving civilization and the way civilization was achieved in this [Andean] area."[1]

> From Lecture 3, on reciprocity and markets: "How far can reciprocity be stretched? What is the size of the unit, what is the complexity of the unit, what are the stratigraphic arrangements, what are the power arrangements with which some kind of reciprocal or redistributive system may be compatible? At what point will all this give way to some other kind of system? This is a very Lewis Henry Morgan kind of question. This is what he was interested in. How did you get to civilization? How did you get to state power? What happened to the earlier ways of organizing human relations?"[2]

---

1. In the second lecture in this volume, Murra refers to two sixteenth-century *visitas* that he edited and published between 1964 and 1972: Garci Diez de San Miguel, *Chucuito*, 1964 and Iñigo Ortiz de Zúñiga, *Huánuco*, Vol. 1, 1967 and Vol. 2, 1972.

2. This volume, page 33.

Murra's Lewis Henry Morgan Lectures are about the Andean "avenue towards civilization."[3] He was intensely devoted to anthropology as a comparative science. In exploring the development of pristine civilizations, Murra established that

> [...] ecological complementarity was a major human achievement, forged by Andean civilizations to handle a multiple environment, vast populations, and hence high productivity. It helps us understand the unique place of the Andean achievement in the repertory of human histories. (Murra 1985a: 11)

In comparison with Mesopotamia and Mesoamerica, the Andean avenue towards civilization is fundamentally different from what has been described for those other two centers of state formation.

I have never known John Murra to read a presentation from a prepared text, either in the classroom or at professional meetings. With a few notes, he relied on exceptional virtuosity as a teacher and on his own sense of theater to reach his audience, forcefully and often dramatically. Thus, in preparing this volume, Freda Wolf and I had only a set of typed transcriptions made at the time from reel-to-reel tape recordings of Murra's Morgan Lectures, together with cassette copies of the tapes provided us by the National Anthropological Archives of the Smithsonian Institution.

We did not edit the transcriptions. We corrected errors made in capturing words Murra spoke in Spanish or in Quechua, and occasionally we filled in a missing word.

This text is meant not so much to be read as to be listened to.

* * *

In 1984, fifteen years after John Murra's Lewis Henry Morgan Lectures, the *Hispanic American Historical Review* published an interview John H. Rowe held with Murra. Rowe asked: "If you were to single out one of your books as your most important contribution to the field, which would it be and why do you rank it above the others?" Murra's reply:

> First, there are interpretative analyses of the Andean accomplishment, among which I find *Formaciones económicas y políticas del mundo andino* satisfactory since it is more up to date, both as to data used and my own ability to fathom the Andean world.
>
> Within that collection, I prefer "El 'control vertical' de un máximo de pisos ecológicos en las sociedades andinas," because it approaches an explanation of Andean success, in circumstances where European historiography and stage-building are rather helpless. Of all my work, this is the essay that has provoked most debate in the Andean countries; "ecological complementarity" may have implications for practical policymaking.[4]

---

3. Murra used the phrase "avenue towards civilization" often during the final arguments of his fourth lecture. He discussed the impact of Morgan's *Ancient Society* on Marx and Engels, as it provided them with an alternative model by which ancient societies achieved civilization, an "avenue towards civilization" entirely separate and distinct from the European scheme with which they were familiar.

4. See Rowe (1984: 644). Murra refers to two of his publications in this interview with Rowe: *Formaciones* (Murra 1975a), an anthology of his articles, and "El 'Control Vertical' de un Máximo de Pisos Ecológicos en la Economía de las Sociedades Andinas", an article that appeared in volume 2 of the Ortiz de Zúñiga visita (1972) and that was republished in *Formaciones*.

Ecological complementarity expresses Murra's recognition of what he considered a pan-Andean ideal of economic self-sufficiency, an ideal achievable by a community's direct control of critical natural resources located within the many, distinct ecological zones that change dramatically with altitude in the Andean vertical environment. Following his painstaking study of two mid-sixteenth-century *visita*s,[5] to Chucuito and to Huánuco, Murra had assembled sufficient ethnological data to represent the social and economic structural arrangements Andean communities originated to realize direct control of a maximum number of vertically ordered ecological floors: the "Vertical Archipelago."

Reciprocity and Redistribution in Andean Civilizations comprises four lectures,[6] organized to examine and integrate the features of Andean social and economic structure that provided a foundation for "success" in Murra's terms: the development of large, dense populations at high altitudes and under extreme environmental conditions, that, nevertheless, formed state, and even imperial, polities. These features include the vertical Andean environment and its rich but discontinuous, vertically-distributed resources (Lecture 1); the socioeconomic "Vertical Archipelago" community structure that provided access to such resources (Lecture 1); the role of reciprocity as fundamental to the successful operation of the "Vertical Archipelago" (Lecture 2); the absence of markets in a system that provided access to far-flung resources as well as reliability of access (Lecture 3); the changing topography of the archipelago and the substitution by the Inka[7] of fictive for consensual reciprocities as imperial devices that altered the ethnic integrity of the reciprocity-based archipelago while conserving the expectations of reciprocity: the exchange of energy as labor by the community in return for often exceptional displays of generosity by the state, largely in the form of feasts and chicha beer (Lecture 4).

John Murra's Morgan Lectures attend to Andean civilizations, although he refers principally to societies inhabiting the steepest and most isolating zones of the Andes mountain chains. These Central Andes are located at equatorial latitudes from roughly the current political border between Ecuador and Peru to the southern shores of Lake Titicaca, on the Bolivian *altiplano*. Except at the choicest of narrow, intermontane valleys, such as those at Cajamarca and Cuzco, Andean topography is sheer and rugged. Verticality is its dominant feature.

The west-east narrowness of the Andean chains and their great height not only produce a steep, vertical gradient, they also generate a multiplicity of compressed ecological zones that change abruptly with altitude (Fig. 1). Overall, the Andean environment is fragile, heterogeneous, and unpredictable,

---

5. Cf. Footnote 1.

6. When reviewing the lecture transcriptions, the tape recordings, and the list of Murra's Lewis Henry Morgan Lectures as advertised in 1969 by the University of Rochester, we found a number of inconsistencies in the lecture titles. We have used the titles that appear on the transcriptions.
    1. (8 April 1969)   The Archipelago Model of Vertical Control in the Andes
    2. (10 April 1969)   Reciprocity, the Anthropological Alternative to Exotic Explanations
    3. (15 April 1969)   The Inca Attempt to Destroy the Markets
    4. (17 April 1969)   Structural Changes in *Tawantinsuyu* Prior to the European Invasion

7. In his book *The Language of the Inka since the European Invasion*, Bruce Mannheim (1991: 235) remarks that "[...] I have for the most part followed the standardized alphabet for the Quechua languages spoken in Peru, adopted by the Peruvian government in 1975, and amended in 1985 [...] It is appropriate for most practical purposes and reasonably approximates the inner structure of the Southern Peruvian Quechua sound system."
    Until 1975, Quechua was written using the Roman alphabet in an Hispanicized orthography. The word Inca was spelled with a "c." The post 1975/1985 orthography alters the spelling to Inka, with a "k." Many authors and scholars continue to utilize the earlier spelling, Inca, but the current, Inka, is closer to Quechua sound systems, which are very different from that of Spanish. In the case of other Quechua words that appear with a variety of spellings in this volume (e.g., *mitima, mitmaq, mitmaqkuna*), for clarification the reader may wish to consult the glossary at the back of this volume.

an exaggerated environment of extremes and multiple stresses. The quality of any of the many and varied vertical ecozones and the stresses they undergo are governed principally by the reduced partial pressure of oxygen and carbon dioxide as a function of increasing altitude; temperature, including extreme diurnal variations and year-round frost at high altitude; availability of meteorological water; soil quality and mineral content; insolation; patterns of evaporation from soils and living things (Thomas 1979).

At the same time, in equatorial latitudes the availability over time of an extreme altitudinal gradient has produced a diverse range of plants and animals adapted to the highly-varied conditions of specific Andean ecozones. Andean flora especially exhibit a high degree of phenotypic plasticity. We recognize, for example, ninety wild species of potato and over four hundred indigenously-named varieties of the common, domesticated potato that flourish from the lowest tier of the *qiswa* rainfall zone (about 2000 m.) up to the *puna* (4000 m.) (Ugent 1970).

The Andes mountain range provides a rich suite of floral and faunal resources that follow a differential, not a continuous, resource distribution. In adapting to environmental heterogeneity and unpredictability, Andean communities depended on a multiple resource base that took advantage of environmental opportunities and minimized risks from perturbations affecting any single resource (cf. Thomas 1979).

The vertical archipelago is Murra's model of the structural mechanism through which a single community controlled access to essential resources that were dispersed among vertical ecozones, often at far remove from the nuclear population. Both the reliability of access and availability of products when they were needed were key. Whether at the level of Chupaychu villages (Huánuco) or the Lupaqa kingdom (Chucuito), nuclear communities ensured direct control of ecological tiers whose natural resources they sought by sending families of their kin from the nucleus to establish permanent colonies in specific, designated ecozones.

Permanent resident outliers exchanged the products of their ecozone with the nucleus. The integrated community was structured as a vertically-dispersed set of islands—islands of kinfolk, islands of production—through which the resources of many ecozones were extracted, processed, and transported entirely by members of a single ethnic group. In the Andes, direct control of a maximum number of ecological tiers by a single community meant sending its people to the resources, not bringing resources to the people; arrangements that normally exist in long distance trade or with the establishment of central marketplaces.

> These ethnic "islands," separated physically from their center yet maintaining continuous social contact and trade with it, formed an archipelago, a typically Andean pattern of settlement. [...] The relations existing between the center and the peripheral islands were those that are called reciprocity and redistribution in economic anthropology. This means that the domestic units devoted exclusively to the herding of camelids in the *puna*, to the cultivation of maize or the gathering of *wanu* on the coast, to timber or the harvest of coca in the *yungas* did not lose their rights to tuber and *quinua* producing lands in the center. Such rights were claimed and exercised through kinship ties maintained and periodically reaffirmed ceremonially in the settlements of origin. Although they were living and working far from the lake [Lake Titicaca], the inhabitants of the peripheral islands formed part of the same universe as those from the center, sharing a single social and economic organization. (Murra 1985b: 16-7)

In his 1972 article, "El 'control vertical' de un máximo de pisos ecológicos," Murra presents schematic diagrams of the vertical archipelago (Fig. 5)—the spatial distribution of the nuclear community and its islands—for the Chupaychu communities (his Case I in the publication) and for the Lupaqa kingdom (Case II). These diagrams, latitudinal cross sections through the Andes mountain range, are slightly re-drawn here as Figures 7 and 9. For each of the two case studies, he identifies the major ecozone occupied by the nuclear community, the primary resources available to the nucleus, the vertical distribution of the permanent outlier settlements, their distances (measured in days-of-walking) from the nucleus, and the resources they provide to the nucleus from the island ecozone each occupies. Murra also indicates in the diagrams that, whereas the nuclear community is "mono-ethnic," or "bi-ethnic" in the Lupaqa-Pacaxe zone, in all cases the outlier islands are "multi-ethnic." Permanency of these outlier settlements was necessary, because often ecological tiers were shared by various ethnic groups, each representing a different nuclear community, and all competing for the same resources—be it salt deposits on the puna or coca fields in the *ceja de selva*— "… in tense but real coexistence" (Murra 1985b: 17).

In 1963 Murra began a meticulous study of the 1567 visita of Garci Diez de San Miguel to Chucuito, located on the western shores of Lake Titicaca. Chucuito was the primary province of the large and rich Lupaqa kingdom prior to its conquest by the Inka and its invasion by the Spaniards thirty-five years before the visita was carried out (Fig. 8). Murra published the entire Chucuito visita in 1964 (Diez de San Miguel 1964), including his critical essay on its significance as a primary ethnological source (Murra 1964).

Visitas—official inspections that Spanish colonial administrators in the Andes instituted during the early, pre-Toledo years of their governance—were carried out by Spaniards who, with prescribed questionnaires in hand, visited communities of various sizes and locations throughout the Andean vertical landscape. Meant as a vehicle for census purposes and to provide the governors with information on a community's taxable resource base, the inspector recorded the responses to his questions made by Andean lords, or peasants, or herders, in their own words.

Garci Diez, a former Corregidor in Lupaqa territory and familiar with the region, inspected the Lupaqa communities town by town. Many of his census questions sought measurements—of time, of space, of people, of herds, of labor owed, of obligations and their reciprocations. Answers were given as numbers. Garci Diez reports an Inka *khipu* that recorded some twenty thousand Lupaqa households, for a population of approximately one hundred thousand persons within the kingdom (Murra 1968a: Table I, 116). Thus, in his 1965 article, "Herds and Herders in the Inca State," Murra was able, for the first time, to use "… raw, first-hand data about particular herds and their herders"; "…a herd of 600 head belonging to a Lupaca mitmaq colony settled in a coastal oasis"; "The 3,242 Lupaca households of the township of Xuli reported a "community herd" of 16,846 head in 1567" (Murra 1965: 188-190).

The visita was new ethnohistoric territory for an Andean scholar. I emphasize the presence of numerical data, of measurements and quantities in the Garci Diez inspection report, because these were direct, on the ground, almost ethnographic data, a rarity in the Spanish chronicles that, prior to the discovery of the visitas, were the historical accounts accessible to the ethnohistorian and the archaeologist. I emphasize this form of data, because Murra did. In 1968, Murra used the Lupaqa visita data to construct a chart (Fig. 14; Murra 1968a: Table II, 129) of the revenues that the two Lupaqa kings of the Qari and Kusi moieties received, province by province, from the labor, the energies of their constituents: revenues in land and peasants to work the land, in cloth "from the Aymara loom," in Indians of service (*mit'ani*), and in *yana* (*anaconas*). For the first time, he (and all students of Andean societies) was able to arrive at realistic measures of labor input, to compare quantities of revenues received and the comparative ratios between Qari and Kusi revenues, to estimate the numbers of animals in the community herds.

The Garci Diez report is still the oldest and most detailed sixteenth-century source for the *Qollasuyu*, the altiplano ecozone that extends roughly from Lake Titicaca to the highlands of northwest Argentina. It provides the best data about the life of Andean herders of the puna.

In 1967, Murra published the first volume of another visita, carried out in 1562 by Iñigo Ortiz de Zúñiga to the Chupaychu, an ethnic group of modest size located in the qiswa zone on the eastern slopes of the Andes, in the province of Huánuco (Fig. 6; Ortiz de Zúñiga 1967). Comparing the populations documented in the two visitas, Murra notes that although they are radically different in size—the Lupaqa kingdom included perhaps one hundred thousand inhabitants, the Chupaychu numbered around ten thousand—nevertheless the visitas had much in common: both provided information assembled in the field from informants whose knowledge came from deep roots in the Andean experience; in both zones some of the respondents had participated in Inka activities at the state level, not only within their own ethnic group; both interviews were designed by the colonial Spanish authorities before the arrival of the Jesuits and the government under Toledo (1570 and later), as viceroy for New Spain; in both cases some of the informants were adults at the time of the Spanish invasion in 1532 (Murra 1967).

> The two visitas complement each other: the chupachu visita has the advantage of providing domestic information, house by house, whereas the lupaqa visita emphasizes the role of the kings. The chupachu spoke Quechua, the lupaqa Aymara. The former had frequent contact with the hot lands [at lower altitudes], the latter informs us about the uses of the puna. The chupachu visita offers more material about the relations between an ethnic group and *Tawantinsuyu* [the Inka state]; the lupaqa visita provides a great deal about the relations of an ethnic group with the colonial European regime. It has been surprising that the two first, detailed sources of this type are so similar at the same time in such clear contrast. (Murra 1967: 383; trans. by HL)

What Murra recognized in his Andean reading of these two visitas was a striking pattern in the way in which Andean peoples structured access to the environmental resources they required. "The desire to control [directly] distant climatic zones through [establishment of] permanent colonies takes the form of a pattern of vertical control that was probably distributed throughout the Andes" (Murra 1967: 384; translated by HL), not only in the regions documented in the visitas. Whereas the Chupaychu visita did not offer Murra the weight of numerical data he was able to chart from the Lupaqa census, it was the careful house to house inspection by Iñigo Ortiz that identified the houses no longer occupied within the nuclear community but that belonged to members who tended distant herds on the puna or who grew coca in the hot lands below. It was the direct evidence provided by the Iñigo Ortiz visita of the deliberate dispersal of Chupaychu members throughout multiple, altitudinal ecozones that Murra recognized as the population-resource structure that also ordered the Lupaqa kingdom.

> The lupaqa state, although centered on the altiplano, controlled many lands in highly varied ecologies with no effort to dominate the intermediate spaces and ethnic groups. Hundreds of kilometers separated its houses in Chucuito from the coastal oases of Moquegua and Arica and the coca fields of Larecaja. Given its much smaller population, the chupachu control of various ecological floors may have been more limited, but their perception of the resources that they believed they required was very similar to that of the lupaqa. (Murra 1967: 384; trans. by HL)

The vertical archipelago constitutes a structure that not only enabled a community's exploitation of resources located at various altitudes/ecozones within the Andes range, it ordered the redistribution of those resources within the archipelagic community, moving it towards realizing the ideal of self-sufficiency. Neither in his first Morgan Lecture, nor in the 1972 "El 'control vertical'" publication, does Murra insist on the essential, redistributive aspect of the archipelago structure.

> The essay I wrote in 1972 in Spanish was meant for an Andean audience familiar with the geography and with previous efforts to understand the achievements of Andean man. My main aim was to offer a contribution to the ongoing debate about the Andean past. I published it for the first time in the second volume of the administrative visita of Iñigo Ortiz [...]. (Murra 1985a: 7)

Murra remarked to John Rowe in their 1984 interview, "Italian and Rumanian versions of this essay have been published, but the English translation has not found a home" (Rowe 1984: 644).[8]

Murra made small, editorial changes to the 1972 Spanish "essay" before submitting it to the Escobars in 1981 for English translation. For his English language audience, Murra was explicit about the built-in, redistributive property of the vertical archipelago.

> Since the idea of some kind of "vertical" exchange is old in Andean literature, this essay has emphasized the redistributive, internal nature of this exchange, rejecting explanations which perceived it as "commerce" or "trade." (Murra 1981: 41)

> Only archaeology can resolve the dating of the early stages of ecologic complementarity. Here I will only repeat my notion that such complementarity is older than the Inka [...]. However, I will insist on my intuitive feeling that the model, though helped by the presence of a strong state, does not require it. I think that the vertical archipelago arose and gradually developed in the Andes as a response to an improved perception of Andean geography and an increased familiarity with the rewards when disparate tiers can be brought together into a single productive and political universe. In lieu of seeing the state as a precondition of the archipelago, I propose that the multi-ethnic productive and administrative experience gained through ecologic complementarity was a salient factor in Andean state formation, particularly when the nuclei were located in the puna. (Murra 1981: 41-2)

The inclusive theme of John Murra's Morgan Lectures links reciprocity and redistribution as those social and economic features that capture most essentially the distinctiveness of an Andean path to civilization. Fundamental reciprocities (*mit'a*) that governed relationships among *ayllu* (lineage) members in small, highland communities such as the Chupaychu, and between the community-at-large and its *kuraka* (headman/leader), functioned to incline the community towards economic self-sufficiency within an archipelago structure of direct control of resources and their internal redistribution. Reciprocal exchanges between members of an ayllu or between ayllus were structured as exchanges of labor time, of energy, not exchanges in kind. Labor borrowed to plow a field or to build a house is returned to the exchange partner for the same or an equivalent service, reckoned in terms of time

---

8. Gabriel and Chavin Escobar translated Murra's 1972 "essay" into English. They completed the translation in 1981, but Murra never published it. The Escobar's English-language manuscript (see Murra 1981 in the list of references) is available in the JV Murra archive at the Smithsonian Institution. (Cf. Murra 1972, 1985a, 1985b.)

and energy expended. By virtue of their membership, ayllu members had a recognized claim on ayllu resources—land, perhaps camelids—and including those resources embodied in the labor services of other members (Murra 1980c). In turn, they owed reciprocal services to those who had loaned their labor. The recipient of a day's labor was obliged to feed those who provided the services and to serve them chicha (maize beer).

> As we can see even from this obviously incomplete list of labor exchanges and reciprocal services *within* the community, the governing idea of the system is labor time. Nowhere [in the Spanish chronicles] is there mention of contributions in kind or in any medium of exchange. The household [no single individual] is the contributing unit and what it exchanges and donates is units of time, labor time. […] Beyond such reciprocity, each household was thought of as self-sufficient and enough access to the society's capital goods was available to make such self-sufficiency at least a partial reality. (Murra 1980c: 92)

The kuraka also was entitled to services, not goods, tendered by the community. He received neither tribute in kind nor compensation. The kuraka was issued a share of land as an ayllu member; he could call upon the community-at-large to work his land and to build his house. In exchange for the services he performed as headman—the systematic reallocation of ayllu land according to the changing needs of ayllu households, protecting the community from aggressive neighbors—ayllu by ayllu, in rotation, the community contributed members as servants for his house, usually old people no longer participating in primary subsistence activities. In return for these community services, the kuraka was expected to provide food and chicha beer to the community several times a month; these were festive occasions (Murra 1980c: 92-3).

The Lupaqa kingdom as documented in the Garci Diez visita of 1567 and that served Murra as a second case study in his analysis of Andean civilizations, was a much larger, stratified society comprised of several ethnic groups and organized by moiety. A polity this large (ca. 100,000 people) was able to support an archipelago of many more and much larger "islands" on both the western and eastern slopes of the Andes. Figure 14 presents the chart Murra distributed to his lecture audience which organizes the revenues of the Lupaqa moiety kings, especially those lords who reigned in Chucuito, as recorded in the Garci Diez visita. The revenues enumerate labor services owed to each lord: agricultural labor, weaving responsibilities, services discharged by individuals in categories such as herding, household chores, labor in the Lupaqa coastal outliers in the Moquegua and Sama valleys, and so forth.

> The revenues are essentially made up of services. What they [the two kings] have is access, differential access, to the energy of different groups in the society. Everybody owes them a few days of work. A smaller group owes them a year of work. Other groups are permanently and in a semi-hereditary fashion attached to particular royal households. […] Clearly, here, reciprocity is very stretched.[9]

Murra argued:

> In a society in which money of universal value does not exist and in which the marketplace is scarce, the only opportunities for inversion reside in the creation of human obligations. That power increased the revenues of the lord permitting him to extend his network of "mutual" obligations to

---

9. This volume, pages 16.

new weavers, farmers and herders, which in turn allowed him to increase the size of his herds and the extent of his lands. [...] To achieve all of this, the political authority put into play its exceptional rights over human energies, herds and lands [...] To discharge and display their obligations of hospitality, the mallku [lords/leaders] needed large quantities of food, chicha and wool. (Murra 1964: 432; trans. by HL)

At a 1983 Wenner-Gren Foundation symposium on Andean ecology and civilization, Murra revisited his, by then, widely read and debated 1972 article, "El 'control vertical' de un máximo de pisos ecológicos en la economía de las sociedades andinas."

> I would like to take advantage of this meeting to restate my original intention: given the scattered geographical distribution of Andean polities, how does one explain that for centuries and perhaps millennia, the seat of power and the highest demographic density in the pre-European Andes are found at altitudes above 3,400 meters? [...] In pre-industrial societies, dense populations are always an indication of success, but how can such density be achieved in *puna* conditions? [...] The answers seem to lie in the high productivity of Andean economies and not of any single region or zone. Still, the *puna* does have advantages invisible to the European eye: here, very early, the inhabitants "domesticated" the cold, thus enabling them to process the many varieties of *ch'uñu* [freeze-dried potato] and *ch'arki* [freeze-dried llama meat] which allowed massive storage of such food for macroeconomic and not merely peasant uses. (Murra 1985a: 3-4)

Murra's penetrating analysis of the Huánuco and Chucuito visitas, following an already encyclopedic familiarity with sixteenth- and seventeenth-century texts chronicling an Andean world seen through European eyes, confirmed the structural features he had identified as fundamental to the Andean vertical archipelago and clarified the Inka state's exploitation of these very features.[10]

> [... in] the century from about 1460 to 1560, which is the one that can be studied in the archives [...] as the Cusco state expanded, the Inka elite (now a set of two dynasties and also a dominant class) carried to the conquered peoples and territories a model of "vertical control" already familiar to most of these groups.
>
> The new scale of operations makes a difference in the content given to the archipelago. (Murra 1981: 42)

---

10.   Murra sets out these features in his article, "The Limits and Limitations of the 'Vertical Archipelago' in the Andes" (1985b: 16-17).

   1.   "Each ethnic group made an effort to control a maximum of floors and ecological niches in order to take advantage of resources that, in the Andean conditions, were found only there."
   2.   "The ethnic authority maintained permanent colonies situated in the periphery in order to control distant resources. These ethnic "islands," separated physically from their center yet maintain[ed] continuous social contact and trade with it ...".
   3.   Members of the peripheral "islands" maintained their rights in the nuclear community through kinship, were enumerated in the visita census, and, together with inhabitants of the nuclear community, "shar[ed] a single social and economic organization."
   4.   Peripheral islands were often occupied by various ethnic groups, each of which represented a distinct nuclear community.
   5.   Reciprocity among ayllu members or between ayllu and curaca or king was integral to the successful functioning of the archipelago. Reciprocal relations always were structured as exchanges of labor/energy and were secured through hospitality by feasting and drinking maize beer. Reciprocities did not include exchanges or tribute in kind.

The vertical control, "already familiar" model incorporated not only the nucleus-outlier direct control of tiered ecozones but the internal structure of reciprocal relations between ayllus and kuraka/king that provided the social foundation for economic success. Most of the innovations made by the Inka state consisted in the utilization and reorganization of fundamental Andean forms of social architecture. Most auspiciously, the Inka institutionalized on a statewide scale long-held Andean patterns of reciprocity and labor services, relying on the older designs of community obligations known and understood by everyone.

The state's rendition of reciprocity took the shape of a corveé labor tax the Inka established to normalize their new relations with the communities they conquered. At least in the highlands, the state alienated from a community those lands the community was not using or could not use, leaving intact agricultural lands required by the community to provide self-sufficiency. In return for the state's "gift" to a community of its landholdings, community members owed labor services to the state. While serving on corvée, no one was expected to supply his or her own support, whether in food, clothing (in the case of the army), agricultural tools, seeds, cotton and wool fibers or any item from the household's resources.

The state exacted three primary and perennial corveé duties from conquered communities: agricultural labor on lands belonging to the state, military service in the Inka army, and the weaving of plain cloth (*awasqa*). Just as in any community mit'a obligations were fulfilled by the household, not by the individual, the household remained the corvée-owing unit to the Inka state. Male heads-of-household could be called up to work in the fields of the Inka and to serve in the army. In both activities, especially agricultural labor, women and children could assist to complete the quota more quickly. Women heads-of-household were expected to weave awasqa cloth—usually clothing for the army—in the confines of their homes. The state provided the cotton or wool fibers, the women provided the labor. The state reciprocated in the same, traditional manner as the community kuraka had, by feeding all workers on corvée and by providing maize beer. Often the scale of state hospitality was bountiful (Morris 1982).

While workers and soldiers were called away, the community tended their fields. Additional corvée duties included public works and infrastructure: building state roads and bridges, especially to accommodate the army, constructing agricultural terraces and irrigation canals required for the state's intensive program of maize agriculture on qiswa slopes, building and servicing way stations (*tambos*) along the roads, storehouses (*qollqas*), fortresses, entire administrative cities, and temples to the Sun (cf. Morris 1993).

The Inka were careful to structure community corvée obligations and state reciprocal hospitalities so that they resembled in form, not in execution, the community mit'a system: [a] people owed only labor time to the state, nothing in kind; [b] the household was the corvée-owing unit; [c] a community's corvée obligations were met on a rotating basis; entire communities were not absent at any one time, leaving some members to care for the fields; [d] agricultural and public works corvée were suspended at critical times in the agricultural cycle, allowing people to attend their fields; [e] the local kuraka often remained in his community and was supported by the Inka in large part to enforce the corvée obligations of his community; the kuraka saw to it that the mandated number of people were recruited and showed up for their labor service; [f] state reciprocity was carried out through feasting and the provision of chicha beer, frequently at generous levels of hospitality. This was fictive reciprocity. No one was fooled. The state relied on the self-sufficiency of the conquered populations in order to inhibit rebellions and to ensure the functioning of the state agenda.

That agenda was sustained by an economy of surpluses that the state stored, inventoried, and redistributed to all workers on corvée and to those who relied on state support: the army, a variety of specialists who became full-time retainers of the state, such as the *aclla* women weavers of fine, *qumpi* cloth and *khipu kamayuk*s (accountants who kept administrative records on knotted-string devices), government administrators, *mitmac* colonists (*mitimae*s), the Inka royal ayllus, royal priests of the Sun, and others. Huge surpluses of food—primarily maize but also tubers—were produced on state lands throughout the empire. Maize was grown on newly-terraced and irrigated fields on even the steepest slopes. As Murra often remarked, "the hillsides were groomed": the sierra was transformed through large scale agricultural programs carried out by laborers on corvée who built the terraces, maintained the irrigation canals, and worked the fields. All this food was stored in provincial state warehouses (qollqa) and in warehouses located at large administrative centers, such as Huánuco Pampa (Figs. 10-13).

State storehouses also stocked cloth. Some held clothes for the army, made by village women who wove them as their household corvée labor obligation. Many others were filled with great quantities of the finest qumpi cloth,[11] woven by aclla (female) and *qumpi kamayuk* (male) specialists who left their communities to weave as full-time state retainers at imperial administrative centers, such as Cuzco and Huánuco Pampa (Morris 1967). Qumpi cloth became an essential and powerful tool of Inka diplomacy, offered as the most highly prized royal gifts to newly-conquered entities. Acceptance of such gifts not only brought communities peacefully into the imperial fold, it established their subservience to the state.

The imperial surplus economic-redistributive mode engendered two state level technologies: storage and accounting. The Inka designed and built large scale storage facilities that, in the puna environment, enabled maize to be kept fresh for as long as four years and fresh potatoes for one year (Morris 1992a, 1992b). Food stored in qollqa at waystations (tambos) along the Inka roads kept the army supplied, and qollqa at large, provincial centers provided the state with flexibility in carrying out its redistributive functions.

The khipu string accounting device was already in evidence within the Wari realm (ca. CE 600-1000) as a modest precursor to the Inka knotted-string design (Urton 2014). At the imperial level, however, the khipu maintained not only the population census of a rapidly expanding state, it also served to record the number of households that owed corvée labor while keeping close track of qollqa-stored items and the state schedule of redistributions from the warehouses. Khipu kamayuks became full-time retainers of the state (Murra 1980a).

The state acted as a market, receiving goods and redistributing them (Murra 1980b). The Inka continued to rely on the self-sufficiency of the communities it absorbed, but the new economic order brought significant structural changes, as Murra describes in his final Morgan Lecture. The imperial archipelago linked "islands" that were no longer distributed necessarily by altitude along a vertical terrain. The state established islands of people in locations it selected according to state resource requirements. Mitimaes (mitmac colonists), for example, were state-constituted groups—in the early years of the empire they were often families located near Cuzco, the Inka heartland—who were sent for a period of two to three years to colonize Inka territories. Towards the end of the period of Inka territorial expansion, the emperor Huayna Capac assembled an estimated fourteen thousand mitimaes to colonize the Cochabamba valley, located on the warm, moist, lower eastern slopes of the Bolivian Andes, for the state production of maize.

> He set up a vast state-owned "archipelago" for the purpose of large-scale maize production, essentially for the use of the army. The work was performed by a multiethnic labor force recruited from a very large area (ranging from the Cuzco region to Chile). [...] Permanent *mitimas* were specifically charged with maintaining the granaries. [...] *Mittayoc* [workers on corvée] rotated on a

---

11. Cf. Murra 1962a and 1975b [1974]. The "Etno-categorías" article is reprinted in Murra's *Formaciones* (1975a [1974]).

yearly basis and performed the heavy work. [They] stayed together in accordance with their ethnic origins and kept their own *caciques* [*kurakas*]; but all were placed under the authority of two Inca governors. (Wachtel 1982)

In other circumstances, mitmac colonists formed garrison-like "islands" among communities newly-incorporated into the state, to replace recalcitrant elements, and to assist with acculturation into the Inka fold. Mitimaes were supported entirely by the state, drawing upon state warehouse resources until they could establish themselves in the new setting.

Murra stresses the state's initiatives in moving groups of people out of their ethnic communities. The mitimaes are one such group. The Cañari military "corps" is another, a single ethnic group of families transplanted from Ecuador and brought to Cuzco where the men provided full-time military service to the royal ayllus (*panakas*). At the same time, the state increased its revenues by establishing retainers to produce goods that were essential to the new economy and political order. To realize the need for enormous quantities of kumpi cloth, not only for purposes of sacrifices but as gifts to military leaders, as gifts to newly conquered communities, for creating alliances, the state established groups of full-time professional weavers for the massive production of the finest textiles. The aclla, young women removed from their ethnic communities, were incorporated into the state apparatus to fulfill the ever-growing needs for the highest quality woven goods.

All these people—the aclla, the khipu kamayuks, the Cañari troops, the mitimaes to a certain extent—Murra argued were removed from their ethnic communities to serve state functions as full-time retainers. Murra saw this as a new and major inroad, promulgated by the state, into the community system of reciprocal relations.

> [...] for neither of the two groups [the aclla, the Cañari troops] is there any kind of precedent in the Lupaqa or the Chupaychu level of magnitude before. [...] At least with the data so far, these seem to be [Inca] innovations. And what's important here—the principle in common—is that [...] you have people who no longer can work in their own community. [...] They are relieved of reciprocal services within their own communities. As the Europeans say, they are removed from the tribute rolls. [...] They no longer owed reciprocal services to the traditional authorities [...] It is this removal, this not being enumerated in the census anymore—that is really important and that creates new people, new energies that can work resources on a full-time basis for the state; and it is this which is new. [...] The break with the kinship reckoning is what's important.[12]

By the time of the Spanish invasion, the empire had achieved its greatest extent. Murra does not dwell on the administrative acumen that held together millions of people over some 4,200 linear kilometers of Andean rugged, inhospitable coast, cordillera, and altiplano. His preoccupation is the turning point when one recognizes the state's manipulation of the very social and economic structures that were the empire's foundations.

Murra cared about and argued emphatically that the Andean case represents:

> [...] a "no beasts [of burden], no wheel" model of achieving civilization [...] It is important to see in the absence of beasts, and in the absence of machinery, the way you are reaching civilization is

---

12. This volume, page 61, 66.

through the manipulation of social and economic categories and the manipulation of people which are, if not completely unique here, certainly have been pushed here with these resources and these circumstances further I think than anywhere else. [...] Finally, when the Europeans come in 1532 [...] we are at the very crucial moment [...] when the old reciprocal and distributive bonds bringing these people together are stretched way beyond anything comparable elsewhere.[13]

One theme persists and provides continuity to all four of John Murra's Morgan Lectures. Advances in any meaningful appreciation of Andean prehistory require the shared perspectives and methods of ethnohistory, archaeology, and ethnology. His 1963–1966 field project at Huánuco Pampa, supported by the US National Science Foundation, included Peruvian and North American archaeologists, an ethnobotanist, an ethnographer, graduate students from Peru and from the United States; Murra served as ethnohistorian. The Huánuco project was an early interdisciplinary effort in the Andes to realize the integrated research approach Murra sought.[14]

Included in Murra's professional archive at the Smithsonian Institution's National Anthropological Archive, there is a two page, handwritten document that appears to be a draft Murra wrote as an introduction to his Lewis Henry Morgan Lectures. The document has neither title nor date.[15]

These lectures argue against a convenience we can no longer afford. Particularly after the Second World War, Andean studies have polarized into two activities conducted by distinct anthropological specialists who were content to withdraw behind the technicalities of their tactics in the field: some, calling themselves archaeologists, concentrated on the monumentality or the earliness of the past. Others, thinking they were doing social anthropology, picked out the contemporary mountain peasant community to stress its isolation or its poverty and how these led to mass migrations to the city.

Thus polarized, neither anthropologist need know anything about the work of the other. Their training was distinct and both were freed from learning the Andean languages—since both activities can be conducted in Spanish. In fact, both can be and frequently are carried on by foreigners.

In recent years, such segmented convenience has been increasingly recognized as interfering with: [1] an understanding of continuity and change in the Andean world, both before and after the European invasion; and [2] the emergence of an Andean approach to the study of what man had once accomplished in this area and of what true options for the future were still available here.

These lectures argue that just as India, France, or China cannot be understood today unless one is familiar with [their] "Indianess," their "Frenchness," or their "Hanness," we must inquire about

---

13. This volume, page 72.

14. The NSF application includes a <u>Short Title of Research Project</u>: "A study of provincial Inca life." The application specifies further a <u>Complete Title of Research Project</u>: "An inter-disciplinary study (ethno-historical, ethnologic, archeological and ethno-botanical) of a specific region in the Andean highlands, that was part of the Inca state and that is described in unusual detail in the sixteenth century archival records" [the 1562 *Visita* of Iñigo Ortiz to the Chupachu]. Monica Barnes notes that later, when Murra wrote about the project, he sometimes included explicitly Quechua linguistics as one of the project's research disciplines (personal communication, 2015). A copy of Murra's NSF proposal is located in the John Victor Murra Archive, Junius Bird Laboratory of South American Archaeology, Division of Anthropology, American Museum of Natural History, New York. Although there is no date on the Museum's copy of the proposal, Barnes estimates it was likely submitted to NSF in 1962. I thank Monica Barnes for providing me with a scanned copy of Murra's NSF proposal. (HL) (Cf. Murra 1962b: 1-4)

15. This document is located among the John Victor Murra Papers, National Anthropological Archives Series VIII, Box 2.

the massive Andean continuities, which I think exist here as in those other foci of civilization. If this is so, the pretense must be dropped that archaeology or contemporary sociology in the Andes can be practiced separately from each other and from history. The heavy overlay of four and a half centuries of mass European settlement and colonialism has no parallel in either India or China; these mask the specificity of the Andean achievement, as they do that of the other Americas.

This preliminary effort, clumsy and stuttering, comes much too early since the masks are so tightly fitted and since we hear so rarely the voice of the Andean peoples themselves. But a beginning must be made, to challenge [the] homogenizers.[16]

* * *

In both his 1984 interview with John Rowe and in his 1985 "revisit" of the vertical archipelago model, John Murra explains that what encouraged him to write and publish the now classic 1972 article was participation in a six-week graduate seminar that Ángel Palerm organized in 1972, with Murra's help, at the Universidad Iberoamericana in Mexico City.[17] In preparing his presentation for the Seminario Comparativo Sobre Civilización Mesomericana y Andina (Comparative Seminar on Mesoamerican and Andean Civilization), Murra wrote what later that year appeared as "El 'control vertical' de un máximo de pisos ecológicos en la economía de las sociedades andinas." Palerm was one of Murra's closest colleagues. Their letters, available in the Murra archive at the Smithsonian Institution, indicate the excitement and energy they brought to organizing a comparative exploration of avenues towards civilization in the ancient Americas. Murra felt safe, challenged yet supported, in that company of colleagues. "I realized that in Mexico I could receive the double benefit of commentaries by the Meso-American participants as well as colleagues from the Andean republics" (cf. 1985a: 6).

Whereas the 1972 article is known internationally as Murra's definitive presentation of the Andean vertical archipelago economic model, he had already presented that model, without naming it, in his 1968 publication on the Lupaqa kingdom (Murra 1968a), using "archipelago" and "vertical control" vocabulary. Naming the model publicly was a Lewis Henry Morgan event—up front, as the title of the first Morgan Lecture.

Murra's 1972 "control vertical" article and his 1969 Lewis Henry Morgan Lectures are not coordinate, however, nor did he mean them to be. The article, written in Spanish for an audience of primarily Andean scholars, offers a crisp account of the vertical archipelago model presented diagrammatically and supported by newly available and, in Murra's hands, singular ethnohistoric data. Murra hid the "control vertical" article at the end of volume two of the Iñigo Ortiz visita. The Lewis Henry Morgan Lectures, on the contrary, were public, presented in English at the University of Rochester to an audience of faculty and students for

---

16.   Murra's final sentence is incomplete. The original sentence reads: "… to challenge those homogenizers who try to … ." We do not have the remainder of the sentence.

17.   The John Victor Murra Papers at the Smithsonian Institution National Anthropological Archives contain various documents pertaining to this seminar. The Murra Papers, Series I, Box 29 include correspondence between Murra and Palerm during the preliminary stages of seminar organization. Box 29 also contains a copy of the seminar announcement issued by the Universidad Iberoamericana. This flyer gives the inclusive dates of the seminar (4 July-10 August 1972) together with a list of the seminar participants. JVM Papers, Series VII, Box 5 includes Murra's handwritten, inaugural seminar presentation on 4 July and his closing remarks on 9 August 1972. The Papers do not include a final list of the participants, but handwritten notes Murra made during the course of the seminar suggest that the initial list of participants named on the flyer had changed somewhat.

many of whom the Andean data and his interpretation of those data were new. Murra's aim and delivery of the LHM Lectures were panoramic: to analyze, then describe the Andean "avenue towards civilization" through synthesis of ethnohistoric data, his broad, personal, ethnographic experience of Andean cultural continuities, and whatever meager data were then available from archaeological investigations.[18]

When John Murra fell ill, Freda Wolf and I decided that we should undertake publication of his Lewis Henry Morgan Lectures. Freda was one of Murra's graduate students in the Department of Anthropology, Cornell University, during the early 1970s. He was chairman of her graduate committee. In 1963, she spent three months in the field as a member of the Huánuco project logistics crew and prepared an index of sites recorded by Iñigo Ortiz in his 1567 *Huánuco visita* to make that document more accessible to the project archaeologists. Freda attended Murra's Morgan Lectures at University of Rochester in 1969. I was an undergraduate student of Murra at Vassar College in the mid-1950s.

In April 2006, I visited John Murra at his home in Ithaca, New York. I brought with me a formal letter for him to sign that authorized Freda and me to prepare his Morgan Lectures for publication. I could not anticipate his reaction to our suggestion. He was thrilled.

John Murra died in October 2006 at the age of ninety. He did not see his Morgan Lectures in print, but he knew Freda and I would accomplish the task honorably. Through the years both of us had become close friends and colleagues of John Murra.

In January 2012, Freda Wolf died at her home in Lima, Peru. We had almost completed a final review of the four Morgan Lectures, had assembled key illustrations, and were about to embark on our introduction to the volume. In a 1996 interview Freda held with Murra in Lima, she wrote,

> Perhaps out of his own personal experience of having grown up in Eastern Europe, a part of the world in which ethnicity was and is a key element in daily life, and because he was able to speak several languages, where others often see the ethnic as a cliché, he sees the world in terms of individuals acting within certain cultural and historical contexts. The ability to put himself into an historical situation or into the description of another society, to understand and to communicate that other situation as a real situation [...] have made him a magic teacher and public speaker. (Wolf 1996: 31-2)

I hope those who knew Freda will recognize her voice in this introduction.

I have been deliberate to communicate John Murra's extraordinary comprehension of the ancient Andean world in his own words. This introduction attempts to contribute a modest structure to the oral version of Murra's Morgan Lectures, a light framework that he would have provided to a published volume. I have especially tried to keep in mind students who read the book and who may be unfamiliar with Andean ecology and prehistory.

There is a host of Murra's students and colleagues, as well as our own colleagues, whom we thank for their help in preparing this volume; Sumru Aricanli, Monica Barnes, David Block, Richard Burger,

---

18.　Archaeological and bioarchaeological investigations that bear upon Murra's vertical archipelago model have tended to concentrate on sites in the lower reaches of the Moquegua valley, in southern Peru. This is the region where the 1567 visita to Chucuito provides testimony, given by altiplano informants to Garci Diez, about members of their communities who live in the coastal region of the Moquegua (Peru) and Azapa (Chile) valleys.

Listed here are several publications that discuss the results of these studies; the earliest became available twenty years after Murra's Lewis Henry Morgan Lectures: Stanish 1989; Conrad 1993; Rice 1993; Sutter 2000; Goldstein 2000; Knudson 2008; Goldstein 2013; Knudson, et al. 2014.

Alejandro Camino, Anthony Carter, Sidney Carter, Sarah Fee, Robert Foster, Thomas Gibson, Paul Goldstein, Robert Leopold, Bruce Mannheim, Enrique Mayer, Perrice Nkombwe, Patricia Netherly, Scott Perrigo, Jorge Recharte, Frank Salomon, Helaine Silverman, Adriana Soldi, Carlos Soldi, Karen Spaulding, Gary Urton, and Judith Willis.

Our special thanks to Robert Leopold who, as Director of the Smithsonian Institution's National Anthropological Archives, greatly facilitated access to the John V. Murra archive, especially in preparing audio cassette tapes from the reel-to-reel original tapes of Murra's lectures. The Murra archive curates transcriptions of all four of his Morgan Lectures. The original tape of the third lecture has not been found.

Shortly after Freda Wolf's death, her son, Andres Romero-Wolf, contacted me and spent several days reviewing all of Freda's computer files pertaining to the Murra Morgan Lectures, which he compiled and sent to me. Andres understood the importance to his mother of the Murra/Morgan project. I remain sincerely grateful for his generous help.

I thank the Reed Foundation, New York, for a multi-year grant in support of the preparation and publication of this volume and the Selz Foundation, New York, for a grant to distribute print copies of the volume to all who helped in its preparation. I thank the Institute of Andean Research for a generous grant to fund the publication of the volume.

Heather Lechtman
Cambridge, Massachusetts
24 August 2014

The Archipelago Model of Vertical Control in the Andes

Four years ago in this very series, Robert Adams[1] expressed quite understandable reluctance at including Andean societies in his comparison of the pristine civilizations [with which] he was preoccupied. You will recall that he compared Mesopotamia and Mesoamerica. But at some point in the very first lecture, he talked about his reasons for excluding the Andes. As I read them, and I was contemplating coming to Rochester, I thought how wonderful, how accurate, how perspicacious those reasons were for omitting Andean civilizations from any comparison of pristine civilizations at this point. The reasons for his reluctance, the factors which made him reject the Andes in his comparison, are as operative in 1969 as they were in 1964. If you remember what Adams [said]—and I assume many of you were here in 1964, 1965 to hear Adams. He made two points: that the [civilizations beginning along the] desert coast of Ecuador, which is the area you see on this ecological map in either pink or red (Fig. 1),[2] which is a true desert and at the same time the home of some very exciting civilizations. These civilizations are known through archaeological work done mostly by foreigners, but the archaeological tactic is unsupported by any historical, any written sources. It is unsupported by any possible ethnological work. All we know is what the archaeological tactic can tell us about these civilizations.

On the contrary, the area in gray and yellow in the middle of this map going from northwest to southeast, the highland area, is very well known from written sources and from contemporary ethnology, but

---

1. "Regularities in Urban Origins: A Comparative Study," Lewis Henry Morgan Lectures, 1965. Published as: Adams, Robert McC. *The Evolution of Urban Society: Early Mesopotamia and Prehispanic Mexico.* Chicago: Aldine Publishing Company, 1966.

2. The map Murra refers to is: Joseph A. Tosi, Jr., *Mapa Ecológico del Perú* (Lima: Instituto Interamericano de Ciencias Agrícolas de la OEA, Zona Andina, 1958). Tosi's map is reproduced here as Figure 1. The map was distributed in 1960, incorporated in a joint publication with L.R. Holdridge, *Zonas de Vida Natural en el Perú* [Natural Life Zones in Peru]; *Memoria Explicativa Sobre el Mapa Ecológico del Perú.* (Turrialba, Costa Rica: Instituto Interamericano de Ciencias Agrícolas de la OEA, Zona Andina. Boletín Técnico No. 5, 1960).

virtually no archaeology has been done in this particular area. And Adams thought this was good enough reason to omit the Andes from consideration and, frequently, as I prepared these talks, I thought how right he was. Nevertheless, this diagnosis which is so accurate is accurate only if we limit it to the two particular tactics that Adams was concerned with: the comparison of written sources with the results of archaeological excavation. I think that if we add some other tactical approaches, if some other anthropological subdisciplines are utilized, we might get more reasons for looking at the Andes in a new way. Maybe not quite Adams' way, but in ways that I think will be profitable in our examination.

In this department, [René] Millon's work in Mesoamerica,[3] elsewhere, the work of [Pedro] Armillas,[4] of [William] Coe,[5] of [William T.] Sanders,[6] of [Ángel] Palerm,[7] has shown us what can be done by combining these two particular approaches. We are far from being able to either have the data that these men in Mesoamerica control, nor can we immediately answer many of the questions that their research raises. Many of these things will remain unanswered in this series of lectures, and just as unanswered in the private, smaller sessions where a man might be more daring, more speculative. We simply don't know enough to answer the kind of questions that the Mesoamerican scholars are dealing with.

However, I would suggest that we have available to us some new approaches, particularly the results of recent research which make it possible, and which encourage us to answer certain kinds of new questions. For example, beyond archaeological excavations and the work in written sources, we have a fact that even I, who [has] worked some time in the Andes, did not appreciate in its proper worth until my very last field trip. And that is the very massive and real continuities that exist in the Andes, between the pre-European period and what is happening there today. Now you would think that if one works on it long enough, this factor of continuities would be one which would [strike] one. And yet, as the years go by and I do more ethnographic fieldwork in the Andes, I am more and more impressed with the reality

---

3.   René F. Millon, archaeologist, who spent his longtime career investigating and mapping Teotihuacán in the Valley of Mexico, was professor of anthropology at the University of Rochester when Murra presented his Morgan Lectures.

4.   Pedro Armillas Garcia, Spanish anthropologist who first defined Teotihuacán as a metropolis. He also worked on Mesoamerican cultivation systems.

5.   William R. Coe, archaeologist and scholar of the Maya, best known for his investigations at Tikal.

6.   William T. Sanders, archaeologist particularly known for conducting an aerial survey of the Basin of Mexico, producing an inventory of sites that had not been studied.

7.   Ángel Palerm Vich was Professor of Anthropology at the Universidad Iberoamericana in Mexico at the time of his death in 1980. In 1936, at the outbreak of the Spanish Civil War, he interrupted his studies at the University of Barcelona to join the army of the Republic. He commanded a division, fought at the battle of the Ebro and in the defense of Catalonia. Badly wounded, he was forced to join the Spanish emigration to Mexico in 1939. Murra, who had left his studies at the University of Chicago to serve as a soldier in the International Brigades in Spain, knew of Palerm and Palerm knew of him during the Civil War, but they did not meet until the 1950s, in Mexico. They remained close colleagues and friends.

Throughout his career Palerm developed a keen interest in irrigation agriculture and especially for its relevance to Mesoamerican cultural development. Between 1952 and 1966 he held a number of influential positions in the Organization of American States (OAS) in Washington, D.C. and edited *Ciencias Sociales*, the journal of the OAS Social Science Office. That office published Spanish and English editions of such anthropologically relevant works as Julian Steward's *Irrigation Civilizations* (1955), Palerm's *Studies in Human Ecology* (1957), and *Middle American Anthropology* (1958–1960), edited by Gordon Willey, Evan Vogt, and Palerm. In 1961 Palerm founded the OAS Department of Social Affairs and served as its director until 1965.

Returning to Mexico, Palerm's goal in the fieldwork-centered programs he developed at the Institute of Social Sciences at the Universidad Iberoamericana and at the Universidad Metropolitana "[…] was to develop an anthropology more closely attuned to Mexican realities. […] [H]e saw anthropology at once as a critical mode of inquiry and as a means for realizing the aspirations of the Mexican Revolution" (Wolf 1981: 612-615). Cf. Victoria Castro, Carlos Aldunate, and Jorge Hidalgo, editors, *Nispa Ninchis. Conversaciones con John Murra* (2000).

of these continuities, and ask new questions of the old material with more confidence in the light of these continuities. We are dealing here not with survivals, we are dealing here not with occasional bits and pieces that happen to survive many centuries of European rule. We are dealing here with real continuities in fundamental and important institutions, such as land tenure, such as the utilization of the verticality in the Andes, the very characteristic features of Andean life—what I call verticality. The use of it, and many other features that I hope to develop for you in the coming series, show that continuities are a real factor and give us results which are not always available, in fact are rarely available, in other parts of the world. We can, therefore, look at the high civilizations of the pre-European period with another dimension to help us.

If you just remember that we are dealing here with eight to ten million speakers of the Andean languages. We don't know how many. This is part of the problem you face when you don't know how real these continuities are and this constant rediscovery of the importance of the continuities—all you have to think is: we don't know how many people speak the Andean languages. Six million, say some, eight million are [sic] possible, even ten million is not beyond [possibility]. And there probably are more speakers of the Andean languages at this moment than [there] have ever been in the last four hundred years, simply because, as everywhere else, more children are alive and those children speak the mother tongue, which means one or the other of the two Andean languages is still spoken by millions of people.

Ecology, agriculture, land tenure. Here are at least three major dimensions in which continuities are not fragmentary, are not peripheral, but at the very heart of Andean civilization then and now. What is interesting is our unawareness, including [that] of the scholars, of these extraordinary continuities. And I think that this unawareness is not just the measure of how little we know; it is a factor, all right. But this is not, I think, the most important factor. It is also how ready the anthropologists, and the man in the street—and by the man in the street I really mean the elites in all the Andean republics—how ready anthropologists and these local elites are to accept the conventional wisdom that the Andean past is doomed if not gone. Even when confronted with the fact that it is not yet gone, the second line of defense, the second line of explanation, of apology, always refers to the fact that Andean civilization is doomed and therefore you can justify your unawareness, your lack of contact, your lack of understanding of this particular human accomplishment.

The second new factor which must be taken into account and which is not taken into account by those who think that it is too early to draw any kind of generalization, is the factor of the emergence of Andean scholars in the study of Andean civilization. This seems to me an extraordinary promising development. They participate in the elucidation of many of these ecological factors that I will present to you today, and Kroeber was actually aware of it. One of the less-known books by Alfred Kroeber, published in 1944,[8] is devoted to a journal, which is his discovery of what happens in the Andes if you accompany a local scholar in the field. You see, many of these scholars do not have the training, do not have the degrees, do not have the kind of credentials that we have come to believe indispensable and the kind of things that Morgan, of course, didn't have. Morgan was his own teacher of anthropology. The Iroquois were his teachers of anthropology, and he taught himself anthropology and made anthropology, a certain kind of anthropology, all by himself. In much the same way, Andean experience teaches people who are sensitive and curious, independently of degrees, independently of professional preparation.

---

8. Alfred Kroeber, *Peruvian Archaeology in 1942* (New York: The Viking Fund Publications in Anthropology No. 4, 1944).

And Kroeber became very aware, as he spent 1942 in the field with Julio C. Tello,[9] he became more and more impressed, how frequently Tello's hunches were right. Tello didn't publish much, and this is what you get from outside scholars. They tell you how little Tello published and how frequently he repeats himself. And the hint for tonight's lecture, to me, comes really from Julio C. Tello's work. When people say that he repeats himself, it is sometimes interesting to see: what does he find interesting enough to repeat, over and over again? And what Tello found important to repeat was ecology, ecology, ecology. Over and over again he came back to the fact that if you are trying to understand the geographical environment and what human beings have done in that geographical environment, you will get no help from published sources. The traditional geographers, traditional ecologists, even the anthropologists will not be help enough. You have to fathom the particular situation on your own. You have to understand it through fieldwork, and over and over again over forty years' time, Julio C. Tello returned to the need to understand Andean ecology if he were going to understand anything.

In a way, what you have developing in the Andes today is something again like Lewis Henry Morgan had. Remember that one of the important things in Morgan's life was his early discovery and friendship with Ely Parker[10] and Ely Parker's family. Parker and his sister lived in Morgan's house and much of the introduction, much of the intimacy that Morgan developed for the Iroquois way came from this proximity, from this tutoring that he received from Ely Parker. In turn, Parker learned about the United States in the 1840s and 1850s in this very area. But Morgan learned a great deal, and in much the same way those of us outsiders working in the Andean area have learned a great deal from Andean scholars and expect that as more and more young Andean people enter the field and bring to it the experience of their elders and their own training, much new information and much new understanding will come through this participation.

But finally, of course, there is another factor which must not be slighted, and that is the conceptual aid which we may receive from the results of modern ethnologic and social anthropological research in [societies] comparable to the Andean civilizations. As opposed to some of the Morgan lecturers of the past, and opposed to some of the writing which has recently come out about Mesoamerica which compares civilizations and is concerned with discovering how civilization emerged in these various areas, I will look for help, conceptually, not so much to the theories elaborated, be it by Morgan and by other followers of Morgan, but I will look for more aid—and in my experience have received more conceptual aid—from the modern ethnologic and social anthropological field work in the Pacific and in Africa where societies, at least to my mind, are comparable and where some of the processes which I have

---

9.   Julio C. Tello, "Andean Civilizations," in *Papers 23rd International Congress of Americanists* (New York: 1930), 259-290; "Origen y Desarrollo de las Civilizaciones Prehistóricas Andinas," in *Actas, 27th Congreso Internacional de Americanistas* (Lima: 1942).

10.   Ely Samuel Parker (1828–95), born Hasanoanda, later known as Donehogawa, a native American of the Seneca Nation, one of the six nations of the Iroquois Confederacy. He was an engineer, an attorney and a tribal diplomat. As adjutant to Ulysses S. Grant, he wrote the final draft of the Confederate surrender terms at Appomatox. President Grant appointed him as the first Native American to hold the post of Commissioner of Indian Affairs (1869–71). He was the chief architect of President Grant's Peace Policy regarding the Native Americans in the West. His friendship with Lewis Henry Morgan dated from the 1840s, when Morgan was often present in Parker's parents' home, where there were discussions and studies among a group of both Native American and non-Native American scholars connected to the group that formed anthropology as a discipline. At the time Morgan was an independent scholar studying the kinship structure and culture of the Iroquois. Parker was Morgan's main source of information and through him Morgan got to know others in the Seneca and Iroquois nations. Morgan dedicated *The League of the Ho-de-no-sau-nee or Iroquois* (1851), to Parker, noting their joint collaboration on the book.

picked for discussion in the series, reciprocity and redistribution, are only some of the many institutional frameworks which would be helpful and which permit us to see the Andes in their own right.

Such things as kingship and the revenues of kingship are things which we can discuss, not in terms of some ideal types set up by what ought to be, but the series of kingships and political units throughout the Pacific and Africa are a very good source of hunches and questions to ask as we approach the Andean situation. Succession in political authority. Status lineages in the Pacific. All these concepts, I think, will be very helpful as we approach the higher civilization of the Andes and it is that which I would like to do with you in this series, to test how applicable they are, to see what kind of insights we get if we apply this sort of conceptual aids to our problem. So what we are doing in the Andes today is combining the two tactics that Adams was talking about, namely archaeological exploration and the use of European written sources, and we add to these two, ethnological investigation of modern, contemporary Andean communities since the continuities are so real, and finally, analytically speaking, we have a four-pronged way of looking at these Andean civilizations. And I think that if we do it in this particular way instead of limiting it to archaeology and to written sources, then maybe it is not too early to draw some kind of a temporary balance sheet and see what we know and what we understand and what questions we want to ask about the Andes.

Let me go back to the continuities I mentioned a minute ago. The main explanation of these continuities, as you would expect, come out of the geographic challenge which the Andes present to man today and all along through the millennium. This challenge Andean man mastered. At the time of the European invasion in 1532, there were many civilizations extant in the Andes, of many different kinds, and we know archaeologically that these were not the earliest states; these were not the earliest civilizations. For centuries, maybe for thousands of years, all kinds of political units, all kinds of civilizations, some with irrigation and some without, had risen and fallen in this particular area. Clearly they couldn't have done it if they had not mastered the Andean environment. But this Andean environment, this Andean geography, was not understood, was not fathomed by the Europeans. They were not very interested in it, and four hundred years have passed and through this period they have tried to ignore it when possible. Sometimes it confronts them and hits them so hard that they cannot ignore it—and then they deny it. It is simply not there. Plans are made, very elaborate, very modern plans, drawn up by the best foreign planners money can buy. And essentially those plans deny the Andean condition. They are drawn up for plants which do not grow at four thousand meters. They are made for roads which have to survive conditions at four thousand meters. So that even the confrontation very frequently is denied, is rejected, by the European planner. And I think this is why so much about the Andes is still misunderstood; so much about the Andes of a very elementary nature which in Mesoamerica, for example, is clearly known, for the Andean area is not yet understood.

The salient feature of this geography is quite simple. You can see it on this ecological map by Joseph Tosi (Figs. 1 and 2),[11] published by the Agrarian University in Peru. Everybody knows about the coastal desert, and I don't talk very much about it. But there is one feature about it which I would like to remind you [...]. The desert does not just stay on the coast. As you can see from the pink and the red, it edges up towards the mountains. It reaches in some places up to eight thousand feet. So if you are going to have human occupation, that human occupation is going to be at altitudes above Tenochtitlán, above Denver. People begin where elsewhere population stops. The most densely populated areas are at eleven and twelve thousand feet. And [in the Andes] human beings normally live at thirteen and fourteen

---

11. Cf. Footnote 2.

thousand feet. Now this is a kind of [challenge], a double [challenge]. First, the desert reaching way up, not just down below. And the very high altitude at which human occupation and civilization have had to function.

Now, the ecological systems which emerge at these altitudes share some of the features which you have met elsewhere. Those of you who have kept up with recent Mesoamerican research in which an interest in ecological features has been one of the characteristics of the work of such people as [William T.] Sanders,[12] the work of such people as [Kent] Flannery,[13] [Richard] MacNeish,[14] have all been interested in what happens and how mountain ecologies are being handled.

I would argue at this first of our four meetings that this is such a special feature—altitude, and how altitude is handled—is such a special feature that we cannot just assume that we understand it from our knowledge of how other people in other mountainous areas, even in our own American continent, have handled this particular problem. And I would like to devote this whole first session to the implications of the kind of ecological systems that emerge here. One thing to remember is, first, that the very high altitudes are combined with a very limited extent of ... arable area. People speak of a two percent area [of arable land], and even assuming they are wrong, as they are wrong about most of these things, suppose it is four percent, suppose it is six percent; it is a very, very low percentage of an immense territory. The map on the board occupies not even half of what I consider the central Andean area, the area of high civilization. A measure of the problem is also that if you live at these very high altitudes, beginning with about nine to ten thousand feet, every two or three or four hundred feet you have a new ecologic floor. There is a new climate, and as you go up these levels are compressed and get narrower and narrower, shallower and shallower. Every few hundred feet you have new ecological conditions, new terrains, new waters, new soils, and in every one of those floors you have to domesticate new crops and find new ways of making a living.

This is present in no other part of the American continent, nowhere else do you have such a dense population at such altitudes, and nowhere else do you have civilization emerging at these altitudes. You cannot get civilization without mastering these very difficult environments, and this is what was done over and over again for thousands of years in the particular part of the world I am talking about.

If you add to altitude all the other factors that have occurred to you—the very abrupt vertical terrain, the slopes, the humidity, the differences in soils and winds, you will get, of course, many more subdivisions, many more microclimates, many more problems for men to face and to utilize and to defeat in order to be able to have civilization in this area. What man is confronted [with] then, is a multitude, literally hundreds if not thousands of quite different pockets. Hidden in particular places in the valleys, up and down the mountain slopes, and in these ecological pockets, over the thousands of years, people developed different ways of life. Virtually everything we are saying can be contradicted with other Andean data. The differences are frequently so serious, our knowledge of the range is so shallow, so superficial, that most of the generalizations that I will present to you in this series for the next four sessions

12.   William T. Sanders, *The Natural Environment, Contemporary Occupation and 16th Century Population of the Teotihuacan Valley* (University Park: Pennsylvania State University, 1970).

13.   Kent V. Flannery, "The Middle Formative of the Tehuacan Valley: Its Pattern and Place in Mesoamerican Prehistory" (PhD diss., University of Chicago, 1964); "The Vertebrate Fauna and Hunting Patterns," in *The Prehistory of the Tehuacan Valley*, Vol. 1: *Environment and Subsistence*, ed. Douglas S. Byers (Austin: University of Texas Press, 1967), 132- 177.

14.   Richard MacNeish, "An Interdisciplinary Approach to an Archaeological Problem," in *The Prehistory of the Tehuacan Valley*, Vol.1: *Environment and Subsistence*, ed. Douglas S. Byers (Austin: University of Texas Press, 1967), 14-24. MacNeish comments: "Thus the ultimate objective of the Tehuacan project was the discovery of processes and causes leading to the rise of primary civilization" (1967: 14).

will probably be contradicted, denied, overthrown within ten years. These are preliminary conclusions that seem plausible at this point. But we are at the very different, very much earlier stage than people in other parts of the world concerned with civilization, and the problem before me is always, "Why is this particular civilization left with so few students?" And I don't mean just so few outsiders because, after all, there are Japanese, there are German, there are French, there are US scholars active in this field. The problem I think, to us as anthropologists, is also why are so few Andean scholars as yet active in this particular field?

How many of these ecologies, of course, we don't know. But the example of the kind of contributions that Andean scholars would make—I would like to mention Javier Pulgar Vidal's work. Back in the 1930s, Pulgar, all on his own, discovered ethnoscience. It occurred to him [...], that the best way to understand Andean ecology, since he couldn't get any help from any published books in Europe or in the United States, was to inquire from the local inhabitants how they classified their geographic environment, what the various climates, what the various vegetations, what the various combinations that existed [were]. He published a book, which, for the 1930s, was a remarkable book.[15] Unfortunately, the various editions that have come out since then include no further work. I frequently urged Professor Pulgar to continue, because it seems to me, if you think about, for the late 30s, for somebody to do what very much later was done, the whole idea of an ethnoecology, of an ethnogeography, appeared only in the 50s in this country. He had thought about it twenty years earlier. And obviously what is needed is the continuation of the kind of work that Javier Pulgar Vidal began at that time.

The Andean accomplishment in this ecological field has long been celebrated, and I don't need to take any time with a group like this to go into any detail. I would like just to remind you of some of the features of it which are important in my thinking for all the future problems that I'll be dealing with in this series. First of all, the domestication of literally dozens, if not hundreds, of high altitude species of plants and the adaptation of the many hundreds of varieties of each of these species to particular microclimates as you go up and up and up and up into the Andes. There are more domesticated animals here than in any other part of the New World. Animals that [carry] and animals that give fibers and animals that can be eaten. Nowhere else in the New World was there such a concentration of domesticated beasts of all sorts used for many purposes as in this area.

I would just as emphatically attract your attention to the preservation techniques in an area in which the climate is so inhospitable the idea of keeping, of preserving food, takes advantage of the local, difficult climate, and the preservation techniques were admirable. In the First World War, the Germans, confronted with a blockade by the Allies, tried to reproduce, in Germany, some of the preserves made of potatoes that are routinely made in the Andes by the average peasant. But of course, the ecological conditions were not the same. *Ch'uño*[16] would never be made in Germany, although they did try very hard. All of twentieth century German chemistry and techniques could not do what Andean peasants had been doing for thousands of years. And with preservation goes the larger problem of storage. If you are living in conditions of such extreme scarcity, one of the things that happens is that the storage processes and the mentality that goes with storage gets a tremendous boost. One of my collaborators in our Huánuco study in 1963 to 1966, Dr. Craig Morris recently wrote a thesis for the University of Chicago in which he dealt with the

---

15.   Javier Pulgar Vidal, *Los Ocho Regiones Naturales del Perú* (Lima: Universidad Nacional Mayor de San Marcos, 1946).

16.   *Ch'uño* is the Quechua term for freeze-dried potato. (Cf. Mauricio Mamani, "El Chuño: Preparación, Uso, Almacenamiento," in *Runakunap Kawsayninkupaq Rurasqankunaqa. La Tecnología en el Mundo Andino*, eds. Heather Lechtman and Ana María Soldi (México: Universidad Nacional Autónoma de México, 1981).

warehouses.[17] It is very hard to convince anybody in this country to publish this particular thesis; I have had no difficulty whatever in the Andes. In the Andes I have different institutions who want to publish it, and not because it deals with storage before the Europeans, but because all the agronomists there hope to use the thesis in the present-day quarrels with the legislature about appropriation. Nothing today compares with the storage facilities that were present before 1500. They hope to use this archaeological thesis as a weapon in their debate with the legislature. This is how real the study of the past is for the Andes.

And finally, beyond animals and plants, beyond preservation and beyond storage, there is the problem of social organization. There are pressures here [in these particular circumstances] in facing these ecologic realities which [push] social organizational techniques, such as reciprocity, to new institutional forms that we may not have seen elsewhere. We get our stimulation from other places where reciprocity coexists with the situation of social hierarchy and social stratification. But the forms, the institutions that arise in these particular situations are novel enough and I plan to devote the second and the third of these talks to the particular institutional arrangements that emerge in this ecological context.

Now, I have no time today to talk about the story of how the vertical control started and how it developed through the millennium. Partly we just don't know [very well] how it happened. And those of you who are interested in knowing what we do know can find it, let's say, in Lanning's book *Peru Before the Incas*,[18] where he has presented quite a bit of information about these earlier periods. The discovery of agriculture, the gradual development of all these species, the slow push higher and higher and higher because this [...] we do know from archaeology, is that as time went by people moved higher and higher and higher. Forced to move, willing to move, we don't know. But the fact is they did move higher and higher and as they went up—the hunter's transhumance that we find in a basin, that we find in various parts of this continent, where hunters [and gatherers] go up and down following the particular [game and] berries and seeds and nuts that ripen at different times, and that Dr. Emma Lou Davis describes so well in *American Antiquity* a few years ago, where she combined ethnographic and archaeological techniques to get at how [...] mountains are utilized by basin people, [Pueblo peoples in the US Southwest in the thirteenth and fourteenth centuries .... so]—that sort of [...] transhumance becomes transformed.[19]

But it changes in a way which is different from the Mesoamerican one and which is particularly interesting, since so many of you are interested in Mesoamerican phenomena: The households and the communities which emerge in these mountains as agriculture becomes more and more important. The ethnic groups, be they large [or] small, continue in their effort which began in hunting in earlier times. And they try to control physically, directly—not through trade, not through specialization in this or that area—but to control direct and multiple access to the various ecological zones that they found useful at an earlier time. The social organization enforces the claims that people make, and they claim as many of these niches as their social organization can enforce. We are confronted here with something that goes beyond seasonality; this is not just seasonal visits to particular places. This is direct control, permanent settlements simultaneously established in various climates up and down the mountains.

17.   Craig Morris, "Storage in Tawantinsuyu" (PhD diss., University of Chicago, 1967); "Storage, Supply, and Redistribution in the Economy of the Inka state," in *Anthropological History of Andean Polities*, eds. J. Murra, N. Wachtel, J. Revel (Cambridge: Cambridge University Press, 1986); "Huánuco Pampa and Tunsukancha: Major and Minor Nodes in the Inka Storage Network," in *Inka Storage Systems*, ed. Terry Y. Levine (Norman: University of Oklahoma Press, 1992a) and, in the same volume, "The Technology of Highland Inka Food Storage" (1992b).

18.   Edward P. Lanning, *Peru Before the Incas* (Englewood Cliffs, NJ: Prentice-Hall, 1967).

19.   Emma Lou Davis, "Small Pressures and Cultural Drift as Explanations for Abandonment of the San Juan Area, New Mexico and Arizona," *American Antiquity* 30 (1965).

Before I go on to some of the details of social organizations that have developed, I thought I'd show you a few slides so you can see the kind of situation we are dealing with.

This is an area, a village settlement, called Cuyo-cuyo (Figs. 3 and 4).[20] It is located at almost thirty-five hundred meters. You multiply—I am not sure I can handle feet so I will explain it to you in meters. And what you have here is literally miles of terracing. This is peasant terracing; this is built with energies that can be mobilized by just a group of villages, very different from state terracing which I will not talk about tonight. And what you have here is an altitude where nothing grows but Andean crops. Potatoes the first year and a whole series of tubers can grow the second year, other tubers which will grow the third year, and then the land rests for eight, ten, twelve years. At this altitude, on these terraces, life is nuclear, as you can see here is a tiny village, up above is another tiny village, there's another one down here. But in this particular area, crops and settlement pattern go very clearly together. These people control not only these higher-than-3,500-meter potato terraces, they also control much of what you see on the next slide. This is physically, literally known. The verticality is perfectly physical.

You see [on this next slide (Fig. 4)], physically the terraces are almost the same. There are small differences which if you are interested in we can talk about, but for all purposes these are the same people, these are terraces in Sandia just below, they are exactly the same community you can see how the houses are distributed. There is no alteration. People lived in their own fields. Throughout the terraces, the very same people owned homes, but here the settlement pattern is different, in this area, which is only a few hours walk, but as many as three or four thousand feet below the previous picture, maize will grow. And the very same community controls both [...].

Small communities of this kind will control directly resources below and above the nuclear settlement. This may mean a day or two of walking up or a day or two of walking below. What you have is seasonal migration with the whole family; children and women and domestic animals, everybody moves from one kind of settlement to another kind of settlement and in both places, the access to land is by the very same community. Many of these cases exist today and in the nineteenth century, we know from historical references, this was the normal pattern throughout. In many places, of course, this is now gone.

You will remember what [William T.] Sanders tells us about a similar arrangement in Mesoamerica. Confronted with this kind of a vertical arrangement, the only options Sanders allows us is warfare or trade. In this [Andean] situation there may have been warfare in the past, but certainly there is [sic] no trade. People repeatedly over and over explain how they don't like to buy and sell; what they prefer is to control directly the resources above and below. We have a very good study done by our Andean colleagues at the University of Cusco. A team went to a village called Q'ero[21] not far from Cuzco and in the village; again,

---

20.   For a discussion of agrarian ecology and the altitudinal zones of production in Cuyo-cuyo, see Figs. 3 and 4, contributed to this volume by Alejandro Camino and Jorge Recharte, that illustrate the Cuyo-cuyo *andenes* in 1978 and 1958, respectively. Alejandro Camino, Jorge Recharte, and Pedro Bidegaray, "Flexibilidad Calendárica en la Agricultura Tradicional de las Vertientes Orientales de los Andes," in *Runakunap Kawsayninkupaq Rurasqankunaqa. La Tecnología en el Mundo Andino*, eds. Heather Lechtman and Ana María Soldi (México: Universidad Nacional Autónoma de México, 1981).

21.   In 1955 Óscar Núñez del Prado Castro, professor of ethnology and archaeology in the History and Anthropology section of the Faculty of Letters (now the Faculty of Social Sciences), Universidad Nacional de San Antonio Abad del Cusco (UNSAAC) led a field research team to the Q'ero region. The team members were: Mario Escobar Moscoso, geographer; Efraín Morote Best, folklorist; Josafat Roel Pineda, ethnomusicologist; Manuel Chávez Ballón, archaeologist; Luis Barreda Murillo, archaeological assistant; Demetrio Roca, assistant folklorist; Malcom Burke, photographer; Demetrio Túpaq Yupanqui, a writer for *La Prensa*. In 1983 Jorge Flores O. and Juan Núñez del Prado B. edited a collection of articles that resulted from the Q'ero research project. The anthology, *Q'ero. El Último Ayllu Inka*, was dedicated in honor of Óscar Núñez del Prado. The prologue to the 1983 edition thanks the ethnomusicologist, John Cohen, for his generous financial support for the

the verticality is even more extreme. I'm sorry I have no slides for you of this particular thing; in fact, I cannot show it. It is so extreme that a man starting from his home at four in the morning will be by noon five thousand feet lower than he started from. And again, in both areas they have houses; in both areas they have fields. And just like the settlement pattern is different at the different latitudes, so is the land tenure pattern, quite different at the lower altitude. And they control both of them. They do not trade back and forth. They do not have specialized groups living in these places. People move, as a unit, up and down, up and down in the season. This is an extreme case, the Q'ero case is a very extreme one, there aren't very many like it. The question is, how prevalent did it used to be, and we cannot answer this particular question.

The case that I showed you on the slides is one not quite so extreme and the distance is not so great. The extremes of climate and ecology are not quite so great. But I would like you to contemplate the possibility of the distances being much greater. What happens when the distances are not literally vertical? In these cases you see the verticality is literal. But what happens when the distances are twenty and thirty days walk away? What happens—let me tell you what happens in this situation is that colonies are set up. Where you no longer can get back and forth yourself you set up permanent colonies of your own people who are there on a permanent basis and to describe it in some detail, let me take some actual cases and discuss [them] with you (Fig. 5).

The real hint for it came from our work in Huánuco. In Huánuco, some of you of course know, but let me say it for those who are unfamiliar with what we tried to do there. We started from a European description of this area, which fortunately for us was not just village by village, but literally house by house.[22] Several thousand houses are described by a European inspector, sent within less than twenty years of the European invasion to answer some complaints by the local people against the European master that they had acquired during the invasion. The witnesses are all adults and many of them were adults at the moment of the invasion. The kind of direct information that you get from interviews with the informants in the city and the very same informants confronted with the situation in their own village, in their own home, encouraged us to go and look through all the tactics I have mentioned: ethnological, crop interest, archaeological, comparative work with societies that we think are of similar complexity but [that] we know from ethnological work. All these various tactics were used.

And as we worked in the area we discovered things we never expected. Most of the plans we made turned out to be too timid, too conditioned by the fact that our training is, after all, from other areas. Even if we don't

---

volume, as well as Edward Dwyer, Patricia J. Lyon, Thomas Müller, John V. Murra, John H. Rowe, and Steven S. Webster for their additional support.

A second edition of the anthology, with additional articles contributed by other scholars, appeared in 2005. Cf. *Q'ero, el Último Ayllu Inka. Homenaje a Óscar Núñez del Prado y a la Expedición Científica de la UNSAAC a la Nación Q'ero en 1955*, eds. Jorge Flores Ochoa, Juan Núñez del Prado Béjar, and Manuel Castillo Farfán (Lima: Fondo Editorial de la Universidad Nacional Mayor de San Marcos, and Instituto Nacional de Cultura, Dirección Regional del Cusco, 2005 [1955]).

22.   Murra refers to the three-year (1963-1966) NSF-funded, interdisciplinary field research project he organized and directed in the Huánuco region, Peru: "A Study of Inca Provincial Life." A central feature of the project was to investigate ecological complementarity and the social and economic organizations that operated within these verticalities among Chupaychu communities described in the official 1562 *Visita* that Iñigo Ortiz de Zúñiga made to Huánuco. Murra published the first volume of the *Visita* in 1967.

In closing the NSF proposal, Murra reviews the project's goals and possible impacts: "Two additional and broader possibilities suggest themselves: 1) the reconstruction of a local, provincial, or to be precise, a peasant version of highland Andean civilization in Inca times; and 2) the archaeological testing of a wide variety of historical and social organizational hypotheses about the Inca state, which cannot be elucidated by any other research technique." A copy of the NSF proposal is located at the John Victor Murra Archive, Junius Bird Laboratory of South American Archaeology, Division of Anthropology, American Museum of Natural History, New York.

want to, we extrapolate. Even if we don't want to, we project what we know, particularly from Mesoamerica, and time after time this extrapolation is wrong. This extrapolation is inadequate. For example, we found the village. In this village, there are papers. You don't have to go to some fancy archive to find a great deal of documentation. After all, these are people who have been quarreling and litigating and fighting, particularly the European settlers in this area, for four hundred years. And they have all the paperwork going back through those centuries, kept, in leather boxes. And if they like you well enough they might let you read them.

In one of these villages [Cauri], we found a paper which dated back to 1585. 1585 is fifty years after the European invasion in this area. And what they did at that time, they went to court complaining that their maize lands were being invaded by other people. We checked where those maize lands are and they are two and a half days away—two days away, let's say, two good strong days away for a strong man walking; particularly walking down it would be two days. And these lands are described by name, and the borders are described, and you then inquire about these borders and yes, every twelve-year-old knows where they are. Every fifteen-year-old has been to all these borders. And we say, "What happens to them now?" "Well, we lost them … ." So I began checking on when did they lose them. They were litigating about it in 1585. They are [sic] still litigating about the very same maize lands in 1825. When you go down below into the maize area itself and you ask: "Where are the Caurino's maize lands?" Everybody can tell you where they are.

"What happened to them?"

"Well, we took them."

"What happened?"

"Well, they no longer come to stay here."

What the pattern had been was, the fact that they were two days away, a very simple village of a few hundred households, no more, was perfectly willing to walk the two days it took and to either settle there permanently or to keep people there long enough to watch and protect the maize crop. And while they litigated about it, they certainly had control of it in pre-Incaic, in Incaic, in colonial, and in modern times. They lost them in very modern times when suddenly it no longer seems worthwhile to walk two days to cultivate the maize field; particularly, if you remember, these maize fields are grown not for food. Maize is not a staple in the Andes. Maize is primarily used for beer and there are, by now, other sources of beer than the beer you can grow.

Cauri and its particular problems allow me to introduce what is really the heart of this whole series. I would like to present to you today and on Thursday at least, if not all through the four [lectures of the] series—I don't know if I dare inflict this upon you, certainly today and Thursday you will have to listen to it—through three steps in the continuum of Andean societies. I would like to present to you three different points in the continuum. I make no pretense that I got the range right. I'm sure I don't have a sample. I'm simply giving you three points in the continuum of how Andean peoples have organized the handling of their ecology today and of some of the social organizational problems on in the next lecture.

The data here is very good and it is based on recent work by my team and myself, and let us have the last slide for just a minute so you can see what the first area looks like.

This is a map of a tiny area in Huánuco (Fig. 6). Its only merit: It is different from all other areas only because this house-by-house description, this house-by-house inspection, these hundreds of pages of interview protocols with the inhabitants in this area were made. And you have here several ethnic groups. The larger one is this one, the Chupaychu. One called the Yacha, one called Quero. The colony that I was telling you about [Cauri] is right here. Their maize is down here. This is about a two days' walk; it's more going up but it's less coming down. And they still come all the time, by the way. Only today they barter for the maize, and that is another story which I will have time to come to in the second lecture. This is the distance that I was just talking about.

I would like now to talk about this particular ethnic group [the Chupaychu]. It is made up in the Inca system of four different subdivisions. One, two, three, four around this particular river, and we are talking only of about twenty-five hundred to three thousand households. This is a very small group. You've seen what they control (Fig. 6). From one edge of the nuclear area to the other within Chupaychu country, what you have is at most a day's walk. The nucleus is a day's walk. But, what is happening here is of course very exciting; it's a rare phenomenon in the Andes. Here Andean crops and maize grow so close together that the nucleus is a very prosperous one, then and now. Of course they have lost a great deal of the lands they used to have down below to European-owned plantations. But still, most of the villages still today have lowland lands for maize and the potatoes are not far away. This is rare, but it happens.

But in addition to this core area, you have a whole series of islands in territories unconnected to this core area (Fig. 7). We are moving beyond the community now. We're dealing with a political unit of a few thousand households that are for example eight, ten, twelve thousand people in the old days. Now, the islands within the archipelago which the Chupaychu control can be briefly listed the following way: Away from this map, three and four days going up, at least a thousand meters, at least three thousand feet and in some cases as many as six thousand feet higher than the particular area we're talking about, they have their herds and they have the salt licks. The herders and the salt winners are settled up there on a permanent basis. They are there full-time and, if possible, they cultivate up there. Their women are with them, the children are with them, and these are permanent settlements. An interesting thing—here the nuclear area is a monoethnic area (all the people in Chupaychu territory overwhelmingly are fellow Chupaychu); up there, the area is multiethnic. The particular resources available at that level are shared by other ethnic groups, some—not three and four days away—but six and seven and eight days away.

And to give you an idea of the continuity that you get in this area, we happen to have a census, not for this area for 1722, but for the upland area. In 1722, 190 years after the European invasion, exactly the same ethnic groups are still up there herding, are still up there winning the salt just as they had done 190 years earlier. These are very continuous pattern[s] of approaching resources, of evaluating resources, and the kinds of things you can do about controlling these resources. But the archipelago is not just made up of that big mainland in the center, and the islands of herders, and salt winners above.

Even more important are islands three and four and five days away below. Downward, where the tropical territory begins and where you begin to get tropical crops, and there are many. But I will mention just two to give you an idea of their differential importance: coca leaf, which you need for many purposes of sociability, medicine, and ritual; and timber. Since most of these areas are above the tree line—there are no local trees in the aboriginal system. Some of the trees you have seen in one of the pictures are eucalyptus. But not aboriginal trees. Down below you have timber and down below you have coca leaf. Plus many other things. Again, down below the islands are multiethnic. People from four and six and eight days away have permanent colonies settled down below and controlling the resources. There is no attempt to control the intervening territory. There is no attempt of setting up what we would think of as a contiguous, continuous [unit]. The Indonesian model, if you think of islands in the ocean which a single political state controls, will come closer to the kind of situation that we're dealing with in the Andes. Nobody tries to control the intervening territory, and of course this raises a problem with what happens to pirates that attack the caravans as they come up and down, and this is a separate problem which I'll leave for you to ask me if you [are] interested. But the archipelago model of ecological islands placed up and down in this verticality and controlled directly by settlements of women and men on a permanent basis. This is the characteristic of so many places in the Andes.

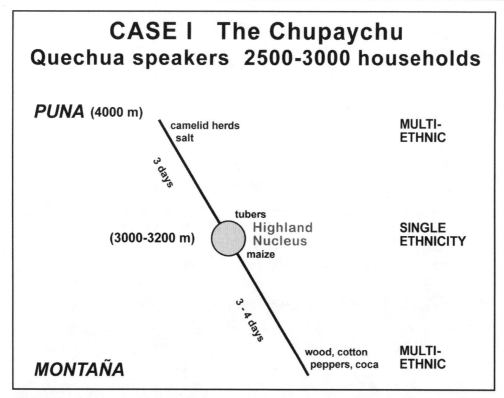

Figure 7. Diagram of Case I, the vertical archipelago model for the spatial and ecological arrangement among the Chupaychu of the Huánuco region (adapted from Murra 1972: 433).

And finally, let me give you just a hint of what's coming in the second lecture. In these outliers, in these islands, people do not lose the allocation of resources which are coming to them through membership in a core group. Be it lands, be it animals, be it people, be it energy, they have full access to all those strategic resources [just as] anybody else who would have stayed back in the core area, all these things are available to them. As the inspector goes from house to house he inquires: "And what happens to the herder?" "Well," they say, "sometimes he comes back, and sometimes his lands are worked for him." There clearly are deviations; there clearly are situations where people don't live up to their reciprocal obligations. And yet it is clearly understood that people away on a permanent assignment do not miss [out] on the allocation of any of the resources that a core inhabitant would have access to.

Let me go to my second step in this continuum. Let us now go from a small area of eight to ten thousand people and jump to a situation where you have twenty thousand households and over a hundred thousand people. This corresponds to another inspection trip; unfortunately, this time, not house by house. I don't know what we would do in terms of size if we had to publish descriptions of house by house for a hundred thousand people, but the description is village by village, town by town. I have published both of these in Peru and they are available to people interested.[23] In this case, let me raise this [map] (Fig. 8) if I can. You will recognize Lake Titicaca on the border between Bolivia and Peru. This particular area right

23.   Murra published the Iñigo Ortiz *Visita* to Huánuco in two volumes: the first in 1967 and the second in 1972. In the first, his essay "La Visita de los Chupachu Como Fuente Etnológica" is included (1967) in a section on "Ensayos Sobre la Visita de Iñigo Ortiz." (1967). In the second, his essay in the section on Ensayos presents his well-known model of the vertical archipelago: "El 'Control Vertical' de un Máximo de Pisos Ecológicos en la Economía de las Sociedades Andinas" (1972).

The *Visita* to the Province of Chucuito, undertaken by Garci Diez de San Miguel, was published in 1964. Murra's essay in that volume is: "Una Apreciación Etnológica de la Visita" (Diez de San Miguel 1964).

here in the very high highland area, close to four thousand meters high, was at European times one of several kingdoms, Aymara-speaking kingdoms, that surrounded this lake. In the recent article in *Ethnohistory*[24] I dealt—in English—with some of these materials, and of course sent them to Weston LaBarre,[25] who had worked here thirty years ago in the field, and he was very interested. He read about it and he wrote me and said, "You know, the Indians kept telling me about the kingdom. But there was no evidence."

The kind of—the effort of destruction, of brainwashing, of impoverishment which has accompanied the four hundred years of European rule in this area would never make you think that there could possibly have been a kingdom of any sort. Yet all you have to do is look at the sixteenth-century churches of the European religion which are standing in every one of these towns. It is those churches that are the real indicator of the pre-European kingdom, because they were built very soon after the European invasion when the resources of the local area were much greater than they are today. And the access of the people to their own resources was much more real.

Let me tell you a little bit about this kingdom so you can compare it with the previous group (Fig. 9). The nucleus is, of course, much larger. We are dealing here with seven provinces, one quite different from the other, but I won't burden you with the details. What you have at the core is different than before. Obviously at these altitudes you cannot raise maize. And they have no maize. But they have a brand-new resource which before was a marginal one, and which now has become a central one; namely, you had immense herds of llamas and alpacas. Individual households will report fifteen hundred to two thousand head. Imagine that what the man reports then and now is rarely comparable to what he really is controlling. The Europeans have heard of individual households controlling fifty thousand head. Even if this is exaggerated, we are obviously dealing here with a very new and very different resource from anything in the center. In fact, herds are really unimportant in the center and north. It is in that area in Bolivia and in Peru that herds have grown so big. And one of the things that I want to take up on in the second lecture is the whole problem of herders when they are no longer two, three, four, seven households going three days away to herd a few hundred head. What happens when the herds are fifty thousand and a hundred thousand? What is the position of herders then, and what is their access to reciprocal services in the communities they come from? But this is really the theme of the next lecture and not today.

One thing you can see immediately, that if you have a kingdom which controls twenty thousand households, over a hundred thousand people, the number of islands in the ecological archipelago will of course be much greater. Many more ecological zones are considered desirable, and the kingdom has the facilities, the energies, to control these particular islands. And in this case, the islands are very much further away (Fig. 9). This zone, between the lake and the sea, can be ten, twelve, fifteen days' walk, depending if you are going down or up; the human being can of course move much faster than a drove of llamas. It depends if the llamas are loaded or not; it depends if they are going up or not. Going up loaded it might take you as many as twenty-five days to get up. It's an enormous distance. The kingdom makes no effort to control the intermediate area, but controls a whole series of oases down on the coast—all the way to Chile and up to about here, all along here. But again, just as we saw in the previous situation, these islands are multiethnic. No effort is made to control either the intervening territory or the niche to saturate the niche completely. There is risk-taking involved. Just like you cultivate in different ways on the slope, so when verticality is no longer literal, so when verticality is no longer geographic, but becomes a cultural approach, becomes a model in

---

24.   John V. Murra, "An Aymara Kingdom in 1567," *Ethnohistory* 15(2): 1968a.

25.   Weston LaBarre. *The Aymara Indians of the Lake Titicaca Plateau, Bolivia. American Anthropologist*, Memoir No. 68 (1948).

their heads; what they try to do is distribute the risks. They prefer to have smaller holdings but in wide varieties of oases to diminish the risk of catastrophe, to diminish the risk of drought, to diminish the risk of hail.

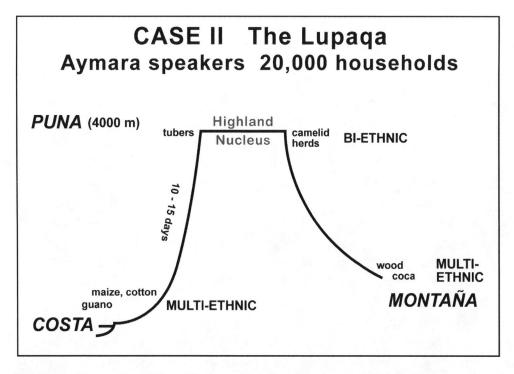

Figure 9. Diagram of Case II, the vertical archipelago model for the spatial and ecological arrangement among the Lupaqa communities located on the western shores of Lake Titicaca and their outliers settled along the Pacific coast, to the west, and in the *montaña* foothills, to the east (adapted from Murra 1972: 441).

And other ethnic groups from above, particularly on this Bolivian side which cannot be seen on this map, another kingdom, the Pacaxe had islands in this oasis system interdigitated with the Lupaqa. But at the level of controlling these lower resources there is again a multiethnic approach. So the pattern remains the same. What you are doing is you are expanding, occupying new territories, a wider variety of territories. These territories can be much further away, but the model is exactly the same. But they don't stop here. The area of the lake is, of course, very, very high. But if you go on the other side of the lake, within three days' walk, four days' walk, five days' walk, you are back in the forest. Much as we saw for the Chupaychu over here, you see—they could get into the green area very fast, just three or four days' walk. So at this area they get into the forest maybe five days' walk away. And there in the timberland, in the coca leaf, in the green they grow maize. I'm sorry, I didn't say what they grew on the oases. They of course again grew beer; they grew maize for beer, and cotton. They grew more maize on the other side, but more importantly, timber, because of course at four thousand meters there is no timber for all the houses, for all the palaces. There was no wood at all and wood is needed and wood is brought, carried on their back, ten, fifteen days away. All these things are described in the protocols of these interviews, and those of you who are interested in details might get them. In both cases, the lowlands on the Amazonic side and the lowlands on the Pacific side are always multiethnic. Side by side, cheek to jowl, different core areas have permanent settlements controlling these areas of settlement. There is virtually no trade. If trade takes place, it is by barter. We can get into this whole discussion in the third session—how much trade, what kind of trade, was there any trade at all? What is administered trade? All that we will look at in the third session.

What is clear here is that there is no attempt of controlling intervening territory. The settlements everywhere are multiethnic. There is no attempt to monopolize the niche once you have some occupation of it and you don't rely on barter. You send your own people as a permanent colony to the newly occupied areas and these people do not lose their reciprocal rights in a core community.

Of course what you are confronted with here is a new phenomenon which was unimportant in the first, Chupaychu case. Here you have real stratification. And this will be one of the factors which we'll have to examine in detail at the next session, but let me give you just a little feeling for what it's like. There is first of all a completely different population present in the area than the dominant group. The dominant group is Aymara-speaking, but there are Uru living by the hundreds and in one of these provinces almost half the population is Uru. These are lake-dwellers who apparently were there before the Aymara ever came. We can't even prove that; this is one of the clichés of Andean life. And by now all the Uru have been destroyed so they will never be able to tell you. But I think there are ways in which we could someday find it out. Then, we have real occupational and status situations as far as the herders are concerned. What is the position of a man responsible for fifty thousand head of alpacas? How are they recruited? How long do they stay up there? We know their families are with them, but is it a lifetime position? Is it a hereditary position? How real is their access, their continued access, to the reciprocal services of their fellow villagers? How real is their access to the produce of land allotted to them by their particular lineage? There are obviously here real problems. There are here real kinks.

In [the] recent article in *Ethnohistory,* I ... published a chart,[26] and if you are interested we could go over that chart, to see the revenues of these [Lupaqa] kings. The revenues are essentially made up of services. What they have is access, differential access, to the energy of different groups in the society. Everybody owes them a few days of work. A smaller group owes them a year of work. Other groups are permanently and in a semi-hereditary fashion attached to particular royal households. Clearly, here you have stratification. Clearly, here you have economic divisions. Clearly, here reciprocity is very stretched. How much reciprocity exists at all? What about redistribution in this particular situation? And fortunately all this new material is now available and I think that in years to come we can get much more about this kind of kingdom, particularly if we get some international collaboration and Bolivian, Chilean, and Peruvian scholars collaborate. Because you couldn't study a kingdom like that, or any of the other late kingdoms, they happen to have resources in what today are three different republics. And the only way to do it is to get the scholars from these various countries to collaborate, to work on this particular thing.

And that of course leaves me only one step in my three-step picture of the continuum. And that is *Tawantinsuyu* itself. The Inca state took and incorporated dozens of groups like the Lupaqa kingdom I just described, and many hundreds of small ethnic groups like the Chupaychu I described a little earlier. It is my suggestion to you that even the Inca state uses this archipelago pattern. They do not control, in any significant way, the intervening territory. Wendell Bennett,[27] [Theodore] McCown,[28] the archaeologists working in the 30s and 40s, constantly kept discovering this archaeologically. They say, "We know from

26.   Cf. Murra (1968a). This chart of the revenues of the Lupaqa kings is reproduced with the fourth lecture (Fig. 14) in which Murra refers to it during his discussion of the Lupaqa kingdom.

27.   Wendell Clark Bennett, "Archaeology of the Central Andes," in *Handbook of South American Indians,* Vol. 2: *The Andean Civilizations,* ed. Julian H. Steward, Bureau of American Ethnology, Bulletin 143 (Washington, D.C.: Smithsonian Institution, 1946); *Excavations at Wari, Ayacucho, Peru* (New Haven: Yale University Publications in Anthropology, No. 49, 1953); *Ancient Arts of the Andes* (New York: Museum of Modern Art, 1954).

28.   Theodore D. McCown, "Pre-Incaic Huamachuco: Survey and Excavations in the Northern Sierra of Peru," *University of California Publications in American Archaeology and Ethnology* 39(4) (1945).

the historical literature that this is supposed to be Inca-occupied, but we can't find anything. There are no Inca remains, where are the Inca remains?" Well, there are no Inca remains because the pattern is still an archipelago pattern. What you try to do is you try to establish in every latitude, and in every situation, frequently for economic and ecological reasons, sometimes for strategic reasons; you try to settle your own people or you try to create in the local situation sources of revenue for yourself, but the archipelago pattern is the dominant one.

At the political level, those of us who are familiar, let's say, with British rule in Nigeria, the whole idea of indirect rule where the traditional elite continues in power, is the pattern used by the Incas as well. Every so often you set up a very large administrative center. The so-called Inca cities, and I will next week, when I'll talk about trade and [reciprocity] and redistribution, I will bring with me some pictures, large-size pictures, to show you some of these administrative cities. There is nothing underneath them [i.e., they constitute a single occupation event]. And they disappeared [were abandoned] the moment of the European invasion. Some of them are in excellent condition for that very reason. They were built for purposes which have nothing to do with the modern Andes. They have to deal with the political organization of this kind of archipelago model. They are strewn through the whole area in such a way as to control. Even new resources which Tawantinsuyu creates: The irrigation or state terracing as opposed to peasant terracing which we saw earlier, or by the alienation of certain resources from the local ethnic community. Throughout there is no tribute. This is a very important difference, I think, from Mesoamerica, a very important factor to understand in thinking about the Andes.

The traditional ethnic leaders in the tiniest group, among the Chupaychu [have access to human energies]. "His wealth," as the Europeans said, constantly surprised, his wealth is in the people that serve him. Everybody owed him a few days and he in turn owed them hospitality, beer, music. As you go to higher groups, again, people have access to the labor of people but by the time you get to the Lupaqa kingdom there are several different kinds of labor and several different ways of gaining access to that labor, because you are dealing with a clearly stratified situation. By the time you get to the Inca state, clearly again the revenues of the state are based by utilizing the services of a wide number of people, but those people never give up anything from their own warehouse. They give nothing of what they have produced for themselves. They give only their labor, only their energy on these islands in the state archipelago, the islands the state has set up. Throughout them, there is no tribute; throughout, there is only minimal and marginal trade. This is clearly a system which must be understood in another way. It is dangerous to apply to it models from other areas. I think it is different enough and special enough to deserve attention in its own right. And in the next session I will continue with this particular thing and see how this archipelago model works itself out and how this continuum of complexity works out within the idea of reciprocity.

Reciprocity, the Anthropological Alternative to Exotic Explanations

In the introduction to this series of talks ["The Archipelago Model of Vertical Control in the Andes"], I concentrated on verticality. This is a shortcut label I apply, at least temporarily, to the Andean ideal of how to handle the very complicated set of ecological relations to which Andean peoples had to find solutions. Now, verticality for me is, then, the handling of this archipelago I talked about [in the first lecture]: how to get [...] access to a maximum of ecologies, and to get reliable harvests under Andean conditions [...] to [keep] the community safe [... in the face of] calamity and disaster. Calamity and disaster, which are quite common in the Andes, and I didn't go into all that in the first lecture. Somebody noted this, that I could have drawn it in sharper color but I thought that maybe you were familiar with some of those things. I indicated also [in the first lecture] that when the political unit grows, something happens to the definition of verticality. As long as we're dealing with the village or a small group of villages in the valley, verticality is literal; namely, gaining access up and down, down and up, to particular ecologies. But when the political unit grows larger and when you're confronted with kingdoms, then the verticality is no longer literal. The whole notion of verticality is expanded, is stretched, and we're dealing with [what] I suppose we could call *cultural* verticality. The ideal is redefined to encompass a vast number of areas and resources very far away, and it need not [...] be arranged in any vertical, physical combination.

Now this phenomenon of verticality has occupied other students, not just those concerned with the Andes. I mentioned [in the first lecture] the whole Mexican approach—[the] Mesoamerican approach. And then as I thought about it, these last two days, it seemed to me I hadn't done enough with it, and maybe the Morgan lectures are not quite the place for it, but it would seem to me it would be interesting to see the difference. And this afternoon Professors [Edward] Calnek[1] and [René] Millon and I had a

---

1. Edward E. Calnek, archaeologist of Mesoamerican societies, focused on the patterns of empire formation in the Valley of Mexico, especially with regard to Aztec imperial bureaucracy. Like René Millon, he was professor of anthropology at the University of Rochester and was present at John Murra's Morgan Lectures.

chance to talk about some of this verticality. And while there is an access to a multiplicity of ecologies in both situations, there are certain very significant differences.

On one level, just physically, the range of ecologies in the Andean case is so much greater. They reach higher, and they also reach to the deserts below at sea level, which again are few and hard to find in Mesoamerica. The range, therefore, is much greater. The inhospitable climate, the inhospitable nature of this range, is also a factor which must be taken into account. What are sometimes in Mesoamerica known as symbiotic regions, in which specialists trade back and forth, up and down, is something you don't find in the Andes. In fact, I don't know how you feel about the whole use of "symbiotic" for human affairs. It may be just a generational reluctance on my part to use this kind of biological terminology when dealing with human beings and human groups. In any case, you cannot really speak of this kind of symbiosis in our situation, in the Andean one.

What we are confronting here [...] is that the same unit, political, a state or village, have this ideal of reaching out and controlling directly through [its] own people, and this is the problem that we are confronting. What is most exciting, and I should have mentioned in the first lecture, and cannot explain why I have omitted it, is the fact that two students of Mesoamerica, Richard MacNeish[2] and Kent Flannery,[3] who have done quite a bit of work in Mesoamerica on just some of these problems, are just now shifting their interest to the Andes. MacNeish is there already at this minute; he went in early March, and Flannery plans to go sometime in 1970 to work on the domestication of Andean tubers. The fact that nobody has really studied the process of domestication gives you a measure of how different, at what different stage, research in the two areas really is.

So, with the coming of these two men, and the kind of interest that I see displayed here at the University of Rochester, I am very excited about what is to come, about the kind of talent, the kind of interest, the kind of questions raised by all these various scholars as they approach with their Mesoamerican experience [about] the kind of situation that Andean man had to face as he built this civilization.

There is one final point about all this that I would like to mention and move on. And that is that both [William T.] Sanders[4] and other students who have been interested in the arrangement of vertically separated regions, have all pointed to the fact that when you are confronted with many different environments, in close proximity, and which are quite contrasting in terms of the resources and in terms of the skills that man must have to handle these resources, they all hope, they all think they might see what they call precociousness in achieving civilization. And you remember the point I made, that one of the groups that I find I can learn most from, are people who sometimes are untutored in formal ways, who lack degrees, but whose life experience in the spectacular and extraordinary condition frequently, if they are thoughtful, reflective people, makes them see very deeply and very interestingly into the problems they face themselves, and they come up with suggestions. I heard this notion of precociousness explained to me at least fifteen years ago by a man who never finished high school—in Andean circumstances. What he lacked in formal training, he had in terms of [...]. [He's] a very good businessman, very practical man who had to handle trucks up and down through the Andes. And as his trucks wore out so much quicker than they were expected to, and he faced drivers and he faced the produce they were carrying, and how

2.   Richard S. MacNeish, "Megafauna and Man from Ayacucho, Highland Peru," *Science* 168 (1970): 975–978.

3.   Kent V. Flannery, Joyce Marcus and Robert G. Reynolds, *The Flocks of the Wamani : A Study of Llama Herders on the Punas of Ayacucho, Peru* (San Diego: Academic Press, 1989).

4.   William T. Sanders, *The Natural Environment, Contemporary Occupation and 16th Century Population of the Teotihuacan Valley* (University Park: Pennsylvania State University, 1970).

marketing was affected by the new roads, it made him think and his thought of this juxtaposition of so many areas is encouraging. Precociousness as encouraging the building of civilization, because you would have to face so many conflicting situations.

Enough for that; let us move on. You will remember that in the first lecture, I suggested that we might usefully look at some recent research in the Andes, at the few moments in the Andean continuum that have emerged in just the last few years, and which might shed some light on the general problem of achieving civilization and the way civilization was achieved in this area. I have put the two ethnic groups on the board here [the Chupaychu and the Lupaqa], and just to remind you I have put a few salient facts. We have the contrast between these two groups: [the Chupaychu], a small group here of a few thousand people, [the Lupaqa], a kingdom here of over one hundred thousand people. The geography is quite different, but what is important is that a community as small as this, made out of a few villages, can control resources three to four days above itself and to three or four days below, reaching out to a variety of microclimates that far away from the center. This is, of course, very different when we reach a kingdom that can mobilize thousands of people and keep them in the field for days, for weeks, maybe for months, and where the ecologies controlled can be as far away as fifteen to twenty days away.

Now, we have here a range, we have here two different instances; now, I don't think this is the range of possibilities. This afternoon Professor Millon frequently asked questions about the irrigated kingdoms of the north coast. They are not fitted anywhere here. I don't know what to do with them, because but for some archaeological information about sequences of pottery types, we know so little about the north coast. We have no ethnographic information. Even the archaeological information is very sketchy, very elementary; there are no continuities. The people of this area were destroyed very early—by the end of the sixteenth century the people were gone. So none of the techniques, none of the tactics that I'd hoped to use elsewhere are of any use here. Clearly, here what we will need is much more archaeology and a completely new approach to the study of archival materials, and I don't see the people who are likely to do this on the horizon as yet.[5] So, I don't pretend I am dealing with the range. I don't pretend I am dealing with a fair sample. All we have is [sic] two instances of some detail that are quite different, quite contrasting, and certain problems that we are interested in might be explained, or might be just hinted at by looking at this material.

Let me move on then, to what is really the topic of today's talk. And which deals with reciprocity. I am interested now in how the social and economic organizations, which operated within and controlled these verticalities, actually functioned. What do we know that is really functional? What can we tell about them as they lived at their own level, since the resources, the crops, and the ecologies between these two peoples are so different? For example: the herds, which in one case are a few dozen animals at the disposal of every village; in the second case are fifty to a hundred thousand head for subdivisions of the kingdom. How many the whole kingdom had we don't even know but it's a very, very large number. And clearly herds of that size must have, must be taken care of by, professional herders. And the whole problem of the social position of these herders, which I raised in the first lecture, is still with us. We would expect, as we see such great differences in climate and the crops grown, we should expect differences in

---

5.   In addition to the work of scholars such as Patricia J. Netherly (a student of Murra; cf. 1978), María Rostworowski de Diez Canseco (cf. 1978), Michael E. Moseley and Kent C. Day (cf. 1982), and Izumi Shimada (cf. 1995), all of which focus on polities located on the central and north coasts of Peru, a surge of more recent archaeological and ethnohistoric studies of north coast societies centers on the Moche. These publications often appear in edited anthologies (cf. Donnan 1978; Alva and Donnan 1993; Uceda and Mujica 1994; Pillsbury 2001; Castillo, Bernier, Lockard, and Rucabado Yong 2008; Bourget and Jones 2008; Quilter and Castillo 2010).

the land tenure system. Access to lands, important in both areas—we should expect significant differences in these rights to land. And we should expect to see differences in ways [of using] the energies necessary to work these particular lands in all these ecologies, the ways of achieving this energy would also be different.

Let me begin with the Chupaychu. In this case, it is very easily seen from the material available to us that in the case of house[hold] gardens, and this can be very interesting but I have no time to describe them, but there are house[hold] gardens cultivated continuously. And also in the case of the maize fields, which remember are primarily for beer-making purposes, not [for consumption] as a staple food. In these situations the continuity of tenure and the continuity of cultivation coincide. The two exist side by side. Year after year the gardens and year after year the maize fields are cultivated without irrigation, and tenure is centered in a different household, and is transmitted within the household. When you are asking how the work is provided, where the energy comes from, there are certain non-accounting systems of reciprocity in which I automatically count on certain relatives, on certain people living nearby, to come and do my work for me if I cannot do it myself. Or just to help me in performing it.

I have put toward the very end, on your right, some of the forms of reciprocity. There are many more, and those of you who are interested can of course go into this whole subject.

But the *yanapa* is an interesting form of reciprocity, partly because no accounting is kept; you assume that over a lifetime there will be plenty of opportunities for people who benefit from your energy today to help you out tomorrow. And [...] the circle of people whom you can count is of course quite restricted. But much of the work is done in this way, insofar as maize is concerned and insofar as the household gardens are concerned.

You also have the second form of reciprocity [*ayni*], and here accounting is kept. Everybody knows very clearly who owes what to whom. And we have the same phenomenon that students of anthropology in other parts of the world have discovered, that men may be quite illiterate but have a marvelous memory for days owed. I was confronted with a situation of this kind when I was in one of the villages in this area, in which the problem came of a young man, twenty-eight, who had left the village when he was six months old. His father had died and his mother took him away, and now he was back, twenty-eight-years old and a father himself. He claimed access to the lands of his father, a man dead twenty-eight years. And I was present when a man was called in, and that man, completely unprepared because nobody knew this young fellow would come back, began reciting the ayni days owed to the dead man of twenty-eight years ago, and all the days the dead man owed at the time of his death. Mind you, this is today in a context where people, everybody in this area has worked in the US-owned mines, everybody has been a trade union member, there isn't a soul in this part of the world who doesn't have a transistor radio. These are fully incorporated into a Western market economy, and even more than that, into a semi-industrial system, because modern mines inevitably are semi-industrial systems. Yet, a man knew what the dead man owed, and what he owed was days of ayni. And what people owed him were days of ayni, and ayni is essentially agricultural work, though it can be used for other purposes as well. And these days of ayni are convertible. You can convert a day of plowing to a day of harvesting. You cannot convert a day of agricultural ayni work to a day of house-building ayni. He also knew, the man, the informant knew, how many days of house building the dead man owed. And it is expected, the young man was asked, "You are coming back, but you're not going to fulfill your father's obligation." And the young man argued that yes, he will, and they said, "No, you won't," and he said "Yes, I will."

But what was interesting to me, is not only that the man remembered, but neither party challenged the authority of the rememberer. It was assumed somehow that yes, he knew, that this was knowable, that this kind of information about days of ayni owed should be relevant to life as it is today by people who have all worked for money in mines. This is a spectacular example, I think, of what I call continuity in this situation. What they were talking about could have taken place as readily in the sixteenth century insofar as it concerns reciprocity—the kind of things I owe and the kind of things that are owed me.

But I will move on from household gardens and maize fields to what is really the most important Andean [concern]. And that is the growing of staple food. That means in the Andes, tubers. Many different kinds of tubers, and the land to which these tubers is planted, that land requires long periods of fallowing. Six, eight, ten years, sometimes even twelve years, the informant will tell you, is how long land should really rest. Certainly six, seven, and eight years is quite common. Here the situation is different. The household does make a claim to certain lands, but since fallowing intervenes, since the land must "rest," as they say, the rights are quite different and we should analyze the claims and how the rights are defended in this situation for a minute. The problem now is to have access to lands, not only in the field cultivated this year, but how do you get access to lands which are resting over a period of four, six, and eight years?

The acreage that is resting—what are your rights to it, and what are other people's rights to the acreage which is resting, particularly as over that period of time people die, young people enter the labor force? There are changes in status which affect your access, as you will see in a minute, to lands. So the moment you have the time coming in, the moment the fallowing, the resting, becomes a factor, you have again tenure situations which we must examine in some detail.

Annually, in high altitudes, a ceremony takes place, and I put the name of it on the board for you, *mananakuy,* or also in some places it is pronounced *mañanakuy.* What happens there is that annually certain new lands; not really new, I should say "rested" lands, re-enter the cultivation cycle. [The earth] must be broken and since the [lands] have rested so long the job is a very difficult one with the technology available, and the part that re-enters cultivation this year and the part that will re-enter cultivation next year, and the part that will re-enter cultivation the third year, are each known as a *suyu,* the second word in that column. And the whole country takes its name from this subdivision. It gives you some of the feeling that people here have for agricultural lands, and for staple, mountain land. The country was known as *Tawantinsuyu,* the four-part place. "Of the subdivisions there are four," would be the closest translation. And what was subdivided were just these pieces of land that gradually enter into cultivation in the ceremonial way in every given year. Ideally, every household controls not one, but several patches in every suyu.

This is, of course, one of the problems that modern agronomists have. They are constantly trying to convince the Andean peasant that they should consolidate. They see in the fact that he has patches all the way up and down this verticality a sign of backwardness, a sign of his unwillingness to really face modern conditions. And he is very firmly convinced that whatever else he is taught, this is wrong. He knows very well that not only do you need access to all these different larger ecological areas, you also within a given suyu need several different patches because you never know where hail will hit, you never know where particular plagues, as they say, will develop. This is clearly related and very sensibly deliberated to the conditions that the farmer in the Andes is facing. Ideally, as I say, we want to control patches in every single suyu. Today, this is no longer true, and I cannot tell you if it was ever true, but the ideal is very clear back then and today.

The land, each suyu, is "thrown" into circulation, as they say; the verb they use is *hitay,* which means "to throw" today, and the ceremonial—I have no time to describe to you but it does exist. Everybody knows which suyu comes into cultivation. There is no surprise about that, and yet it is felt that the entry, or the re-entry, of this land into cultivation, is a matter for ceremony, is a matter for ritual observance. And this is true of maize and tubers both. But there is considerable difference. Maize is treated much more matter-of-factly, because even if lost, the loss is not as important, not as great as that of the tubers. In the case of the tubers, the authorities of the community and in the past, the important leaders, not just community leaders, but the leader of all the Chupaychu was expected, or at least some authority is supposed to come and be hospitably received on the patch itself. Anybody else, any adult can come, today, till today, too, and then, [...] what they all do, they drink, they chew coca leaf, and they walk around the patch. It's a public recognition that this man has made a claim, the claim is recognized by all, and it is done in a ceremonial, ritual context. And this is also the time when new claims can be stated. You see, because inevitably six, eight, even ten years have passed since the last time this particular place has been cultivated. And meanwhile any number of people have grown up. Some have died, some have gone away. New claims are staked out at this ceremonial moment. And the most obvious one is of course the major status change in the Andes, which is marriage.

It is at marriage that the new household is formed, and a physical house is built. And full adulthood is reached at the moment of marriage by both women and men, and that is when you stake out your claim to lands to be grown to staple food. There is almost no inheritance. The early Europeans are constantly surprised by the fact that people don't inherit. And of course the reason for it is that you "inherit" but at a different moment. You inherit when you need it most, when you are setting up a new household and when you want access to the strategic goods of your culture. Claims are made from birth. Made on your behalf, if you're a baby, by your kinfolk, by your parents and your kinfolk, but none of these claims are as important as the one that is made at the moment of marriage. So you have all the old claims reiterated and publicly recognized. You have all the new claims made and satisfied, particularly if your kinfolk are strong enough and if you can enforce the claim you've made. But even outsiders, and I have seen situations in which, let's say, the local parish priest, the local policeman, people just temporarily thrown into the community, will come at mananakuy and make a claim. They aren't always satisfied; very frequently [in] modern times the feeling is that the pressure of population is so great that there is no land for these strangers. But on occasion strangers have also been granted a piece of the strategic resources of the community.

There is an interesting point here, which—an Andean writer whose name I have put at the extreme left, Guaman Poma,[6] who was an Andean man who wrote in the early part of the seventeenth century when he was quite old, and what he wrote took the form of a letter to the king, a twelve-hundred-page letter to the king of Spain, telling him about all the things the Europeans had destroyed in this area. And asking the king to create a new, what he thought was a good government. It's a good story but we're late and I can't tell you the story. But the important thing is that he has worked for a long time with Europeans. He has been an acolyte to a variety of European ecclesiastic types, and he knew what Europeans said about Andean folk, and it's relevant to this claim. He says the Europeans are constantly accusing us of having no charity; that we have no orphan homes, no old people's homes, no asylums for those who are weak and powerless, and he said that in Peru we don't have any of those things. And then he goes on, much as an anthropologist would today, to explain why we don't need any of those things if access to the strategic goods of your culture are readily accessible to everybody and you gain access to

6.   Felipe Guaman Poma de Ayala, *Nueva Corónica y Buen Gobierno* (Paris: Institut d'Ethnologie, 1936 [1613]). Also: Felipe Guaman Poma de Ayala, *Nueva Corónica y Buen Gobierno*, John V. Murra and Rolena Adorno, eds., traducciones quechuas de Jorge L. Urioste, (México: Siglo XXI, 1980 [1615]).

these resources continuously. Just by being alive, just by being present, you are constantly inching your way towards more and more resources and a maximum point is reached at marriage and as you have children, and then gradually as you are older and don't need as much, you will have less. This whole situation of no charity, of no inheritance, of this funny system, constantly bothered the Europeans who had to confront it in the early century, and will be one of the reasons that you will see why so many exotic explanations have crept up in anthropology and outside it. It is so odd, to untutored Europeans who come out of a market economy and who have such a different approach to what they consider important.

How much should a household have? And I put on the board another word in the Andean languages, which is an important one—*tupu*—because that is the measure. And again the Europeans constantly ask, "How much is a tupu?" And nobody can ever answer it properly because it is the wrong question. Tupu really should be *tupuy* which is the verb "to measure". And you should get as much as you need, depending on if you're a new household, depending on how many children you have, depending on what floor in this verticality you're talking about. Because the necessary tupu at one level is much less than it is elsewhere. Up in the staple food area, the tupu is of course much larger, because you must allow for all those years of resting. While down below where things are grown annually, clearly the tupu is smaller. By now the Europeans have actually managed to transform the tupu into a measure of surface, but it is very difficult to see how they could have done it before present conditions. In the old days it meant just as much a surface as the linear [measurement]. They would say how many tupu there were along the road. Tupu is also the amount that a llama can normally carry. It clearly has to do with something else. And unfortunately I cannot tell you all the different things it has. I know some of its characteristics, but even I, looking at it for years, have not been able to really fathom this situation. It measures, but it measures many things having to do with human welfare, and with ideal human expectations. It isn't very much to say that, but that is what it does, it does not measure surfaces. Whatever I don't know, one thing I do know—that the European way of using it will not work. And again, we come to the situation which Andean people, who have had no training, can explain it so much better than people who are confronting these situations without the proper breadth of cross-cultural perspective.

In 1713, a man called don Guillermo Gato,[7] a man from this area, is trying to convince the Europeans of how this works. And page after page after page of explanation which I wish I had time to read to you, but, you will have to take my word that it is quite interesting. The most exciting aspect of the discovery of our fieldwork in Huánuco in the last few years was to discover that mananakuy, which was primarily known in the south, in the Cuzco area, is unknown in places where I did my fieldwork, but a variety of it appears. What is known as a suyu in the south turns out, in Chaupiwaranqa, to be a *manay*. And a manay is a subdivision of staple land that comes into cultivation in any given year. And manay is a very interesting verb. It is a verb, again, which Europeans had a terrible time translating, and one of them finally says, exasperated, "It is to ask when you are sure to get." And this is so very representative of Andean reciprocity.

What is, after all, reciprocity? If you are delivering the energy, if you are delivering the resources, this is obligatory. This is aid you are giving, resources you are giving; it is obligatory. This reciprocity has

7.   Guillermo Gato, « Declaraciones de Don Guillermo Gato, » in *Visita y Composición que el Marqués de Valdelirios, Juez y Visitador General de Tierras, Hizo en Términos y Juridicción de la Ciudad del Cuzco, 1711-1714* (Lima: Archivo Nacional, Títulos de Propiedad, cuaderno 454). This testimony is cited by María Rostworowski de Diez Canseco (1964). Some of this discussion by Guilllermo Gato is reproduced in Marco Vinicio Rueda and Segundo Moreno Yánez's *Cosmos, Hombre y Sacralidad* (1995: 184-85, 192), where it appears in a reprint of the 1968b article by Murra, « La Papa, El Maíz, y los Ritos del Tawantinsuyu, ». We thank Frank Salomon for providing these references to Guillermo Gato's testimony.

nothing to do with personal generosity. It has nothing to do with hospitality. It is a compulsory thing. Now if you are thinking of it in terms of services, then of course you say, these are the services I must give, this is a question I must answer. The energy to work these lands is of course an important part of reciprocity, because not only do we get access to land in the particular way I have described, but the lands are worthless if we don't have the energy to work them. And there are many different kinds of services, many different kinds of work, and I have no time to go into it in detail. Enough to say that reciprocity, or as they would say, the loan of certain services, because they think that the service is being loaned, since it will be returned in very similar services; a day of ayni will be returned in a day of ayni, and very clear standards as to what a day is—on both sides. And these are granted according to kinship obligations; these are granted according to rank. Because both kinship and rank considerations do come into it and should be taken into account.

One thing the beneficiary must always do in *all* the systems of reciprocity, because there are many more than the three I have listed, there are dozens, and some have disappeared. Some no longer can be studied today. We know what they were in the past but all my questioning has never brought any response about these particular systems. So we can expect at least half of the different kinds of reciprocity to have disappeared, partly, of course, because the kinship situation has also been very Europeanized. But there is one thing that is common to all these systems: that the beneficiary must provide hospitality, and the hospitality is not the minimal kind. It is always, and should always be within a festive sense. There should be music, if possible, there should always be alcohol, there should always be coca leaf. It isn't, just, you know, a plate, a cold sandwich thrown in. This is hospitality you're offering; this is a reciprocal thing, and the food should be elegant, the food should be better than what you would normally eat by yourself. You offer more, and what is an appropriate reciprocal gesture at this level is very well understood by all parties.

Those away in other ecologies, those who are not present, those who are up above, those who are down below, all keep their reciprocal rights in the original community. They keep the rights in the energy of others, and they keep the rights in resources themselves. Their lands are worked for them while they are away, and they get the produce which has been harvested and stored for them. They may have to come and get it; sometimes it is delivered to them. There are many differences here that don't matter for our purposes today. But, their fields are worked and their kinfolk watch it so that this obligation is really performed, and what is more, rank authority, the people in charge politically at this level and not at the very topmost level here, but among the middle levels down here, their leaders list this obligation as one of the earliest obligations they have, to watch that the rights of the absent, those who are performing these vertical duties for the rest of us, should get what is coming to them. This is a very interesting thing because we come back, of course, to these exotic explanations we'll see later on. The fact that things are done, that things are watched, that you do get access to things which are coming to you even though you are absent, impressed the Europeans so very much. And the very fancy explanations that then emerge to how it really works or why it should work or what analogies from European life can be found to explain it.

Let us look more carefully at this situation. Let us now introduce another variable which I have mentioned several times but haven't looked [at] with care. Let us introduce now rank and political authority. How do they fit into the reciprocal picture? At the Chupaychu level, you have at least three levels of authority: the two men who were the leaders of all the Chupaychu, another level down below them immediately, and another local, village level. In all cases where we have anything as to what was happening in the sixteenth century we know that, [in] quotes, "everybody" came to help out, and in turn the authority which was benefiting sponsored the hospitality—for hundreds of people in this case. There was enough beer, there was enough coca leaf, there was enough food, for hundreds of people to come and work. Not very much, just a few days every year, some say two days, some say three days, and we don't have to go into the details of that. The fact is that everybody owed services and everybody was fed in a festive spirit and the music played all the time.

The lords in this situation have one other thing which I mentioned in the question period [in the first lecture]. The lords are some of the very few people who are polygynous. They have access to the energy and to the son-producing capacity of three, four women in a society in which the bulk of the people are monogamous. They have, overwhelmingly, one, two, three retainers. Some of these retainers are vertically invested, but some of them are right in the village and their services are an important part of the ability of the ethnic leader to perform his part of the reciprocal obligation.

One important thing, that of weaving, [with which] I have dealt [...] in an article in the *American Anthropologist*;[8] it is a very important aspect of reciprocity because cloth was the object of highest value in the Andes. The greatest artistry was involved in the weaving and therefore all the social obligations surrounding the giving and receiving of fibers and weaving were very important. Enough to say at this moment that, although the authority benefited from the weaving skill of both men and women, the authority always provided the fiber from its own storehouse and this fiber was woven in their homes by the people in the community. Observe an interesting thing: the form of no-accounting assistance, the simplest form of reciprocity, what [Marshall] Sahlins[9] would call "generalized" reciprocity, in which you make no effort to keep track—yanapa—reappears in a very odd situation. The *yanapaqkuna* are the retainers. The "q" here is the person who does it. It's an action, sort of like tailor—"-or" or "-er"—in English. "Kuna" is simply the plural; you don't even have to use it. The *yanapaq*, the helper, is in this case not just a helper without any accounting, without any quantification; on the contrary, this is the first, frequently, in a hereditary condition of dependency; a hereditary retainer. Again, this is a large problem of the retainers, and I'll come back to it in the fourth and last of these talks, because it is a very important whole issue with the position of some students of the Andes who look at slavery as one of the exotic explanations of the system. But I think it's important to note that the most prevalent, the most household, the most kinship-oriented type of reciprocity ties in with dependency, sometimes hereditary dependency. The political authority has claims, which it can enforce, most of the time, to the resources, and these resources from everything we can tell are much greater than those of the ordinary household.

And here we meet one other form, one other social position in the system, which again is constantly giving trouble to the Europeans. The *waqcha* is a person that has struggled getting the reciprocal services or the reciprocal resources due him. The Europeans are constantly translating this as "poor." Until today, in Andean speech, waqcha means, in ordinary translation, poor. If you begin to examine it a bit you begin to see what it really is with the informants who know, or looking at the old dictionaries, and it disappears. It becomes the widow, it becomes the orphan, it becomes the person that doesn't have enough relatives to really make in loud tones and in an assertive way the claim to the reciprocity which is due them.

I can move much faster now because on this model everything else is built. When I come to Lupaqa, the society is much larger. As we saw in the first lecture, there is real stratification; there is ethnic stratification since there are several different groups within the kingdom and there are people who are captives and come in from someplace else. There are many more retainers. The situation is very much more

8.   John V. Murra, "Cloth and Its Functions in the Inca State," *American Anthropologist*, New Series, 64(4): 1962a.
9.   See Marshall Sahlins, *Stone Age Economies* (Chicago: Aldine-Atherton, 1972), especially, Chapter 5: "On the Sociology of Primitive Exchange."

complicated. But some things are clear. The political authority, the man of rank; in this case, the lord, the kings of this situation, have access to lands and to herds in every one of the seven subdivisions of the core areas of the Lupaqa, and then they have access to resources in all the outlying areas where the Lupaqa felt they had to have resources. The Lupaqa king, like the Chupaychu senior man, has access to everybody's "energy" for a few days. And there are long descriptions of how festive this opening of the agricultural season was because everybody, including the lords, was out in the fields and the drums were played, and the music, and there was plenty of beer and coca leaf was passed around from hand to hand. And the work is then in this context.

But you have at this level one group of people which do not exist here.[10] These are people, in the case of the upper moiety king there were sixty; in the case of the lower moiety king there were forty-seven; young men, unmarried, but fully vigorous, fully grown, who owed a year of services to the kings and would then return to the community and would marry. This is very different from services owed by everybody. These are only sixty out of what, fifty thousand? But still, these are people whose energy is somehow appropriated by the political authority for a very long period of time. And apparently the primary purpose to which these men were used, in addition to agriculture and herding, was in the job of droving. You had to go up and down with the caravans of loaded llamas, down to the coast, inland into the forest, and this job of responsibility for them [was] maybe even a soldierly duty. The European documents are not very clear about how the caravan was protected as it moved along this vertical axis. And apparently one important function is the protection. Anyway, these men are a new feature in this more complicated political system. Finally, these fellows [the Qari kings of the upper moiety], just like these [the Kusi kings of the lower moiety], have full time retainers, some of whose sons inherit the dependent position of their fathers. So we have here a variety of categories. In both situations, though, the moiety provided for the people working for them, and what they provided was not just minimal food, but in a pattern of hospitality, in a pattern of festivity. Because it keeps, no matter at what level you are dealing with, the expectations of those performing the service. It is not just a situation in which you would fulfill an obligation. It is an obligation in the context in which you are fed, and the situation is ritually and from a fun point of view, a real one.

Let me now shift levels again and leave these two situations behind, and come to the kingdom itself, to the Inca State, Tawantinsuyu. How much of this picture is still operating? What is new when you reach instead of just a hundred thousand plus; when you reach five million, six million? An immense territory reaching all the way to southern Colombia and down into northern Argentina: millions of people in such a broken terrain; so difficult to put together even today, and very difficult for them to put together because they were constantly facing rebellion. Now what happens when this political organization gets so big? And remember that I am using this very large state as if it was the first, but there is no reason to believe that this was the first true political state. I just don't know about the other ones. The chances are very good that partial consolidations had taken place before. Archaeology frequently points to what John Rowe calls "horizons," when certain kinds of archaeological remains are much more widely distributed and we assume that because of this wider distribution you actually have political controls.[11]

---

10.   Murra refers to a chart he mentioned in Lecture 1 and will discuss at length in Lecture 4. It is reproduced here in Fig 14. The chart indicates the relative revenues, primarily in the form of labor, that the two Lupaqa moiety kings received annually from the communities within the kingdom.

11.   John Howland Rowe, "Stages and Periods in Archaeological Interpretation," *Southwestern Journal of Anthropology* 18(1): 1962.

Now, as you get to this larger situation, what is happening? The state did claim its revenues to support the bureaucracy, to support the army, to keep armies in the field for months at a time. And the armies were very large at this point since they were continuous, annual wars. The state pretended, the state claimed that its exactions, its demands made upon the citizen, were nothing but the traditional patterns of reciprocity writ large, involving many more people. But no more was asked of them than the Chupaychu senior man did in a tiny situation, and in the Lupaqa kingdom a slightly larger situation. What they pretend they're doing is the same thing but the demands are spread; the demands are projected. Since at the local level, reciprocity involves energy, not goods; at the royal level, the Cuzco level, what the state claimed was energy and not goods. You don't have tribute in this situation. This is a very important difference from the Mesoamerican situation. You don't hand in goods, you don't hand in anything that you have produced yourself. You have complete control of what you produce for your own household, for your own larder. What then do you owe? What forms does the owing of energy really take?

And I think this is an important thing, because we must see this verticality model and reciprocity within the context of the truly political unit of this enormous size. And what is happening is apparently simple, maybe too simple. And this is where the danger is. To allow these energies an arena for productivity, the state sets up islands—to continue with my metaphor—islands of resources throughout this immense territory located in many different places at all these different latitudes and altitudes. These islands of resources are set up just like the Chupaychu did, just like the Lupaqa did, by sending out colonists from a central place, who go into an area, occupy it, hold it, and make productive whatever resources were there. But the immediate question is: Where do the resources come from? Inevitably much of the resources come from alienation of local resources. Lands, waters, herds, are alienated from local populations as part of the initial battle, as part of the initial war, and particularly if these peoples rebel later on then they pay for their rebellion by having more and more of the resources alienated from them. And under the pretext of pacification, islands of resources are set up throughout the kingdom.

The interesting thing is that when the early Europeans in the sixteenth century talked to these populations, everybody said, "Yes, these are royal lands. But these are our lands." Everybody clearly remembered that this had been alienated. The pretexts that this is how the kingdom has right to some of these resources were very well distinguished by the local people. They did know. And I don't think there is any reason to think that the local populations believed the fiction which governed, that this was somehow a form of reciprocity as well, or only a form of reciprocity. Finally, not only were there colonists, not only was there alienation of local resources; a very important point is the creation of local resources. The state can mobilize so much larger units, not just of soldiers, but also of civil engineering workers, people who can build roads, people who can build terraces, people who can dig irrigation canals. Vast numbers of people can be mobilized for two and three months a year. Not more than that; but still, two or three months a year if you have thousands to mobilize is of course an enormous resource, and these resources, then, were created.

The best example here is, of course, the monumental treatment of land. State terraces are true monuments, and are built much as palaces or temples would be built. And those of you who have ever seen in the Andes, let's say, the terraces of Yucay, know that here is a temple, here is the monument, and the only thing to which the monument is built is the fact that you have created a terrace, that you have been able to terrace a hillside and all the benefits that terracing brings everywhere in the world. These islands of the state are worked just like we saw with the different resources available to authority before. They are worked, quotes "by everybody." Everybody is liable to do some of the work, and the work still takes place in an air of festivity, music is still expected to be provided, a king is expected to provide food and drink, and these islands of state resources set up everywhere are worked by the local population in a very complicated system of taking your turn, along, again, both kinship and ethnic lines.

Had we the time we would go through some of the details. What the people working expect are the status goods that they have expected all along. We have situations in which people rebel, because they did not get what they should be getting, and the rebellion is, again, you could predict, almost, if you know very little about the Andes, you could predict what they will want: maize to make beer and cloth. What the authority, the generous, hospitable authority benefiting from this kind of reciprocity does is be generous with the things that people have not much of, maybe maize, and beer, because it's associated with festivity, and of course, cloth. Cloth, cloth of all kinds; this is the lubricant of all social relations, but particularly when social relations are in the hierarchical context. Everybody gives and receives cloth all the time. The gods receive—a hundred garments are sacrificed to the gods every day in the capital. So, with the gods you offer just what you would want yourself, but when the situation is a hierarchical one, that is when cloth is given away continuously and when cloth is expected.

Throughout this system there is no tribute. You never give anything from your own warehouse. You give only your energy, and this is not complete and this is in a way false, because there are exceptions. You never give anything that you have cultivated or made yourself, from your own things. But you do give, and this is a need to research which I think should be done which I haven't been able to do as much as I would like to with it; there is an expectation to turn over all wild things: the eggs of ducks from Lake Titicaca islands, feathers, very special feathers of particular colors, which all boys out birding must remember to bring back at the end of the season. Certain wild products like bee honey, and later in European time, wax. All these things which are wild, that nobody takes care of, that are the result of nobody's foresight and provision, these were expected to be handed in in kind. And the very fact that you have these exceptions, I think, highlights the fact that you give nothing else that you yourself grow and produce. But it does not explain these exceptions. I think the exceptions are something to remember. And finally, one other thing is given in kind, and that will be the theme of the fourth talk, namely: while you don't insist as a state on the local citizenry turning over anything from your own larder, what they do turn over is themselves. While there is no tribute in goods, as time goes by there is more and more tribute in people. There is a certain people and I think a growing number of people are plucked out of their ethnic and kinship unit and put to work on a full-time basis, therefore with completely new status and a completely new context as full-time state retainer, and the word used for them is the same concept we have met already. They are helpers. Clearly "helper" here means something that we must examine, because you're doing it all your life, and at least some of your children will be doing it long after you're gone, but the word used for them is the same one throughout, [yanapaq]. The continuities through all these things, the marvel that was built here by them, I think, is a very important one.

To give you a hint about the wild things, there is an element which I haven't mentioned yet, that the legal fiction is established in which all resources, all the lands that me and my kinfolk normally control and leave to each other and give to each other, all those resources are defined in theory as the state's. And this fiction has much utility in justifying many of the things that the kingdom wants to do.

What the state did with all the things it gathered, what the authorities at this local level and this intermediate level did with all the things that were produced by this energy, is of course the topic of the third talk, the next talk, when I will deal with redistribution, the opposite side of the kind of situation that I have dealt with today.

You will have noticed that this picture presented to you today is different from that which you will find in a large number of books which are available about the Andes, in paperback or even in hardback edition. So much is written about the Andes, and I think what they've been puzzled, trying to understand how year after year after year, popular books come out, frequently with drawings by Guaman Poma, which are excellent; four hundred—twelve hundred pages is the whole thing, of which of the twelve hundred pages, four hundred pages are drawings. They're marvelous, constantly reproduced by all these popular editions. The books sell very well; the von Hagen book sold 400-plus, thousand copies.[12] It is spectacular if you think about it. But you see from what I tell you how little we know. Most of the things I told you are the results of the last two year's research. They didn't even have that five, ten years ago. There is this interest, these books are coming out, yet we are confronted with so little information. How do you bring the two things together? And here is where the title of this talk that Mr. Harris[13] referred to comes in. Here is where the exotic explanations come in. We know so little, but we know certain things, and those things, since we can't stand not explaining them, to say, as I say, that I am ignorant, and that I want all of you to come in and help me with this research, because obviously I cannot do it myself. For one thing, every year it gets harder and harder to move at four thousand meters and be active when you get there. I first went to the Andes when I was twenty-five and it took me a few weeks to get used to it. In recent years it takes me longer and longer and longer and I can foresee that I might have to stop at three thousand meters. The next piece of the verticality will have to be somebody else's. Yours, preferably.

What is happening here is really very crucial. Something attracts the attention of the European mind and has for centuries now. There is something about the systems in this area which makes people wonder, which makes people insist on an explanation and they will not tolerate the notion that we don't know enough to give an explanation. I remember when I was writing my thesis some fifteen years ago on the subject. I was researching everything written about it and I found a whole book in which the author, a North American, was explaining in great detail how Sir Thomas Moore's *Utopia* was based on the Inca system.[14] Now there are certain difficulties with it, you see, because Sir Thomas Moore lost his head in the year that Pizarro invaded the Andes. (Laughter) But, no, no, no…no no no. You see, once when in exile, Sir Thomas Moore was in a Dutch tavern, and in that Dutch tavern he heard a man explaining *Utopia* to him, and that man, much earlier in 1502, in 1503, had been in a, in a sea, in a shipwreck on the Brazilian coast, and there heard, thousands of miles away from the Andes, about the kingdom which was not only rich in cities and gold, but where welfare and social justice prevailed. Where people were happy. Where all the needs were satisfied. And this idea had travelled clear across the whole Amazonic forest to shipwreck itself on the same Brazilian coast. Well, this is a bit difficult thing to argue, either pro or con, since I can't prove that he didn't hear the story, but it shows you the level of the discussion.

If you think of the more serious of the books that have been written about it, which is Baudin's book, *L'Empire Socialiste des Inka,*[15] which has been translated and which is still worth reading because he worked very hard and was a very serious economist. He was a conservative economist, and he tried to prove just the opposite. He tried to show what happens when socialism prevails: how regulated people are, how everything was figured out for them, what they would do, who they would work for and how they would get what they need. He thought this was a horrible situation and that this is what the Incas

12.   Victor W. von Hagen, *The Desert Kingdoms of Peru* (London: Weidenfeld and Nicolson, 1964).

13.   Alfred Harris was the head of the anthropology department at the University of Rochester from 1964 to 1971 and the editor of the Lewis Henry Morgan Lecture series from 1962 to 1989.

14.   Arthur E. Morgan, *Nowhere Was Somewhere: How History Makes Utopias and Utopias Make History* (Durham: University of North Carolina Press, 1946).

15.   Louis Baudin, *L'Empire Socialiste des Inka* (Paris: Institut d'Ethnologie, 1928).

were all about. He attributed the welfare features to the benevolent kings, and it is interesting to see the conservative French professor of economics matching what is essentially the ideology of the Inca elite. Because this is what the Inca elite told had happened to the Spaniards at first asking. These fellows were a bunch of savages. They had nothing. All they did was fight each other. We came in and made peace and we civilized them. We taught them how to do all these things. Now you and I know that archaeology can point to most of these Andean features being thousands of years old, before the coming of the Inca. But the Incas say it and I'm sure some of them even believed it.

The interesting thing is that there are people among us who are so ready to accept this kind of an exotic explanation. It seems to me that with all the talk about Utopia, all the talk about socialism, my own early definition of the system—I am in print in a book you cannot even hope will go out of print that people will forget you ever said, in the *Handbook of South American Indians*[16]—I talk about the feudal quality of this particular society, and those of you who've been involved in the recent debate about feudalism in Africa that Jacques Maquet started a few years ago[17] will recognize some of the reasons why I have long since taken back—except I can't take back that page from all the handbooks.

The most recently interesting exotic explanation is, of course, Karl Wittfogel's.[18] Wittfogel in his book on Oriental despotism allows how the Inca State was not a classic case of Oriental despotism; he thinks of it as a loose Oriental, because of course there is little irrigation in the islands where all these societies emerge. But, there is very real irrigation dependence on the north coast. And I am quite convinced that he has an important thing to say, where you have large scale irrigation, where there is no alternative but to rely on the deep canals, and the canals were very complicated, those of you who have read [Paul] Kosok's work,[19] where he shows—it's so curious that nobody has followed his research. He has been gone for ten years now and his research was done even ten years previous to that, but nobody has followed up and it's not hard to do. He showed how, in the old days, the waters from several different valleys could be thrown according to need from one valley into the other. We can't do it today. We cultivate much less land today than they did in 1500. So clearly irrigation here is a terribly important thing, and the kind of rigid social structures that depend on irrigation are important. But when you say that this whole system I have described to you is somehow a loose Oriental form of despotism, it seems to me that the only, simple explanation of reciprocity stretched—of reciprocity applied by rank and class, to new situations, maybe not doably, maybe not forever, but at least the attempt is made by authority to stretch in its own benefit—the whole notion of reciprocity is a less exotic and maybe useful hypothesis for work.

I don't want to leave this forum without reminding you of one important piece of work by John Rowe.[20] Fully twenty years ago, John Rowe pointed to such obvious things but that nobody had seen before. That the Inca system is described to us by perfectly reliable Europeans as being governed by an administrative decimal system, in which units of tens, hundreds, thousands, ten thousands, were organized for administrative purposes. The only trouble with it is that you never find it in the south, where the Incas came from. You never find the decimal system in Cuzco or in Puno or in Bolivia. You only find it in the center and north. And what Rowe suggested is this decimal system is too rigid, too arithmetic,

---

16.   John Murra, "The Historic Tribes of Ecuador," in *Handbook of South American Indians*, ed. Julian H. Steward, Vol. 2, The Andean Civilizations (Smithsonian Institution, Bureau of American Ethnology, Bulletin 143, 1946).

17.   Jacques J. Maquet, *The Premise of Inequality in Rwanda* (London: Oxford University Press, 1961).

18.   Karl A. Wittfogel, *Oriental Despotism: A Comparative Study of Total Power* (New Haven: Yale University Press, 1957).

19.   Paul Kosok, *Life, Land and Water in Ancient Peru.* (New York: Long Island University Press, 1965).

20.   I have been unable to locate a publication by John Rowe in which he makes this observation. Whereas Rowe is known to have held these views, apparently he never published them. (HL)

to have been a highland thing; it was maybe borrowed from these coastal kingdoms when these coastal kingdoms were incorporated into the larger [entity]. It makes perfect sense to me. This is just the kind of thing that was possible. This is an idea he threw out twenty years ago. It has brought no echo; I cannot understand why people wouldn't work more with this sort of thing. I think that this can be done. There are these eternal puzzles as to why we try to write and give those fancy explanations all the time and don't do the simple research that can be done. Some of it is just pencil and paper. I don't think these are accidents. I think there is a perfectly sound explanation which will bring it all together.

But let me mention just one more exotic explanation. And that is one which has now grown very popular because it is the official position of the Communist party in the various Andean countries. The official position now, it didn't used to be this but just in the last few years, is that the old system I have been describing is a slave system, and what we have confronted here is a slave economy. The same man, Emilio Choy,[21] who knew all that about precocity, and knew about it fifteen years ago before the anthropologists did, Choy is one of the people, there are many more, who have argued in print as to the best explanation here is to take out of the stages suggested by Lewis Henry Morgan and by Engels—[take] slavery out as a possibility and to describe the Andean system this way. I will not go into it today because I will devote virtually the whole of the fourth session to this particular problem, but I would like just to see the multiplicity of what I call exotic explanations. Feudalism, socialism, slavery, Oriental despotism, so many different suggestions have been made in a situation where we are really at the very early simple-minded level. We need the simplest kind of description of the ecology and the plants. We want to know more about the rainfall. We want to know more about how long land should rest. We want to know more about reciprocity and labor. We are confronted with a situation where, for four hundred years, real continuities in this part of life have been present, and accessible to field work by anybody here who is vigorous enough to go up and down terraces.

In this southern situation, the yearning for exotic explanation is what must in turn be explained. I hold no brief for this particular thing. This is useful in these very early stages. As time goes by it'll probably be no good and we'll throw it out. Figure out something better. But the search, the yearning for exotic explanation, is something that within the sociology of knowledge deserves some attention and the problem really to think is: "What would happen?" Suppose reciprocity as an explanation to all this is omitted. Suppose reciprocity is wrong. How would you explain the particular facts, which after all are available to everybody? Some Lupaqa and Chupaychu are fairly new but even they are now printed so anybody can get at the information which is available. As I have said before, I am much more impressed with how much help an explanation like reciprocity which comes out of, after all, out of fieldwork that people have been doing in the last thirty, forty years in the Pacific and Africa, where at least in my mind, societies of comparable complexity of enough similar organization do exist and where reciprocity and redistribution can be fitted in with differences in rank and even with political and economic stratification. In that sense I am much more of a comparativist; I am looking at situations elsewhere in the world today which can be reached through modern anthropology, not through some kind of elaborations that have to be invented.

Well, I see the time is up and some of these thoughts that I planned to present to you maybe can be postponed or maybe will come up in a discussion. But I think that I do want to leave a question with you. How far can reciprocity be stretched? Or, another way, when does reciprocity give out? When do

---

21.   Emilio Choy, "Desarrollo del Pensamiento Especulativa en la Sociedad Esclavista de los Incas," *Actas y Trabajos, Segundo Congreso Nacional de Historia*, t. II (1962).

the exploitive elements within reciprocity, combined with stratification and hierarchy, when do those exploitive elements get to be stronger? At what point does reciprocity lose its elasticity? Because obviously, reciprocity can be stretched. It has a give to it. But the give is not eternal. At some point it will no longer work. At some point the exploitive features will destroy it. And to this topic I will devote the whole fourth session, and I think I can leave you here, but I would like you to think about it for [the] next [lectures].

The Inca Attempt to Destroy the Markets

[In the first two talks of this series, emphasis] was centered upon reciprocity and the allocation of access to land and to human energy. I spent a lot of time describing all the various ways in which energy and land were allocated, and characterized the particular way these could be achieved as reciprocity. I also talked a good deal in both sessions about the various ethnic groups that underlay *Tawantinsuyu*, the Inca state, and gave it its particular flavor. I did both of these things because it would have been very hard to develop the later points which come [in this and the next lecture] unless we got away from the received conventional picture of civilization in the Andes—one dominated by an all-powerful state and then all those exotic explanations as to why the powerful state did what it did with its power. And secondly, the unawareness of the dozens and dozens of ethnic groups, large and small, that continued to exist and function very effectively, very meaningfully, underneath and within that overall state picture.

The fact is that these ethnic groups are thoroughly recognizable. They are very readily seen the moment you take a look at them in the early years after the European invasion, and really all the way through until the nineteenth century. Today they are harder to see, but in the nineteenth century they were very readily apparent, visible to anybody who cared to take a look.

The reason, as I say, that I did it this way, is because it goes against the prevailing viewpoint on these peoples, and most progress in research has been done in this area. In many other aspects of Andean studies, there has been relatively little progress. But whatever progress has been made in the last ten years, let us say, has been in these areas to understand how reciprocity worked, in what institutional form reciprocity is visible, and secondly, the recognizable and functioning ethnic groups within the state.

Now, in these coming two sessions, I would like to shift away from that emphasis, and do, in a way, what I have neglected to do all along—go back to more conventional, more traditional ways of looking at Andean civilization. The emphasis will now be on Tawantinsuyu. What was the Inca state like? How was it organized? I will be using materials from these recent researches whenever they seem to be relevant, but the emphasis will be much more traditional. I will ask questions about the state, how the state functioned, and specifically, on the economic organization of this political unit.

The question that I left you with in the preceding lecture is still with us: How far can reciprocity be stretched? What is the size of the unit, what is the complexity of the unit, what are the stratigraphic arrangements, what are the power arrangements with which some kind of reciprocal or redistributive system may be compatible? At what point will all this give way to some other kind of system? This is a very Lewis Henry Morgan kind of question. This is what he was interested in. How did you get to civilization? How did you get to state power? What happened to the earlier ways of organizing human relations? What replaces a reciprocal, redistributive system? Because no doubt about it, I may have underemphasized it in the second lecture, but I certainly don't intend to do it in a real way—it was a tactical arrangement of things. I do not mean to de-emphasize the truly stratified way in which this society, the last of the states, was organized. It is only the last, it is not the first. Many other states had existed in the Andes and our knowledge of them is much more fragmentary. So while I will frequently be talking as if I were dealing with the earliest or the only, I know all along this is not so, and in a research situation, if we stayed together for a long piece of time, we would have to face the fact that many other states had arisen and fallen in this area before.

The Andean civilization we meet at the time of the European invasion is to my mind still very much within the reciprocal, redistributive arrangement. It is stretched; there is a great deal of tension within the system. And the whole [fourth and final lecture] will be devoted to these tensions, and to the kind of institutions which emerged reflecting the internal strains and internal tensions. But at the moment we meet [Inca civilization], insofar as we understand its functioning at all, these early reciprocal and redistributive institutional arrangements are still fully functioning. They are not just something claimed by the elite, by the ruling people in Cuzco. This is not just some fiction. The Inca lords come to the people they have incorporated into their state and claim it. This is truly an operative affair, and the easiest and quickest and best way to see it is to notice that although the state was very real, and the kind of chores the ordinary citizen was obligated to perform by the state were again, very real. All the way through the revenues of the state were not based on tribute. There is no tribute. The peasant, the individual, the members of the various ethnic groups incorporated into the state, do not contribute anything from their own household. Their own granary is not emptied. You do not have to give up what you yourself have produced. It is because of this that I thought that, instead of talking about it, I might pass out among you a list of things [contributed] by a small ethnic group, the same group I referred to in the first and second of these lectures, the Chupaychu—a small group, a few thousand households.[1] Ideally there should be

---

1.   In his publication of Volume 1 of the *Visita de la Provincia de León de Huánuco en 1562*, (1967), the Iñigo Ortiz inspection of the four *waranqa* of the Chupaychu, Murra included an earlier, 1549 visita to the Chupaychu that Marie Helmer had published in 1955-56. (Cf. Footnote 3). Murra drew upon the information contained in the 1549 visita to assemble a "list of things contributed" by the Chupaychu that he distributed to the audience at his lecture. In 1549 the Chupaychu claimed that, at the time of the Inca, they numbered four thousand households. When asked about what the Chupaychu gave to the Inca, the visita records a long list of services, including laboring in the imperial gold and silver mines as well as services provided in Cuzco, such as sowing fields that belonged to the Inca, weaving cloth, herding llamas, providing the skills of carpenters and potters. They gave only services in labor to the Inca. In response to questions about what the Chupaychu give now, at the time of the inspection, to the European *encomendero*, they cite cotton clothing that they make and contribute every fifteen days, many sacks of coca leaf every three months, and a long list of products such as honey, cakes of wax and salt, sandals made of *cabuya*, maize, potatoes, and animals: chickens and sheep. In addition to these goods, they give agricultural services to the encomendero, men and women to weave woolen clothing, fishermen to provide fish, and so forth (cf. Visita de la Provincia de León de Huánuco de 1562, 1967, t. 1: 305-308).

four thousand households, but in practice, there are not. There never have been. There certainly are not four thousand households when we first meet them seven years after the invasion.

Observe an important thing about the date, at the very top—1549 is literally only seven years after the coming of the Europeans.[2] To my knowledge, nowhere else in the Andes, do we have anything this early or this detailed. We did not have anything this detailed for any other part of the Andes or for any other period. No informant here has yet been baptized. By the next inspection, in 1562, all of them, particularly the top men, all have European names. At this point, all the witnesses still have their Andean names and none of them are baptized.

Seven years after the coming of the Europeans, I submit to you is a remarkable way of reaching into the past, and figuring out what the system was. Now, I do not think the actual quantities are very important. Several scholars confronted with this list immediately began their arithmetic and added up the numbers and of course you end up with four thousand people, and ideally there are only four thousand households in this area. And I do not think there ever were four thousand households. So I would not worry too much about what the figures mean. Sixty people to do this thing, two hundred and forty people to do something else, sixty men to watch the dead person of the king, two hundred to accompany him, to carry him in litters and hammocks—that is not the important thing. What is crucial is, first, the focal thing: all the things put together are all contributions of energy. What people are giving is [time]. Not a single one of the items on the list is something that people contribute from their own larder. All of it is a matter of labor.

On the very next page, in the very same document is a list (which I did not burden you with, but anybody who wants it can get to it) is a list of what they gave to the European *encomendero*, to the European who ruled their lives at the time this inspection was made. There you have a blend of actual commodities contributed as well as time. But in this list, it is clearly only one principle that governed, and the various chores are, of course, very interesting and if you want, during the discussion period, we can talk about the list. The [name of the] person that first stumbled onto this document as part of a long process of litigation over land is at the left of the board, a French historian [Marie Helmer[3]]. And she published this particular document, and it has since been republished and it is now very readily available in this publication that Professor Harris has in his office.[4] And if you are interested, we could look at it.

Secondly, this is important—besides the fact that everything is a contribution in energy, look at the very bottom of the list. At the bottom of the list you have the largest number of people: two items of five hundred each. And those are really the most important ones, not only quantitatively because more people work at it, but because from everything else we know about the system, this is where the important contributions are. First of all, all the people working, cultivating, for the king on all the king's estates, on the "islands" that the king sets up in the various ecologies and in this area, which is, by the way, if you are interested in where it is located, it is in this particular valley, right here, sort of in the center of Peru, and looking toward the Amazon, but still quite high. These five hundred men, and it does not matter if there were fifty or five hundred or a thousand, the numbers are unimportant, but a large number of people for a community this small work annually in the islands [of resources] producing revenues for the state. At first glance, these are the most important things. Second, is the second from the bottom of the list: the

2.   1549 is just seven years after the "pacification" imposed in Huánuco by the Spanish-Huanca alliance.

3.   Marie Helmer, "La Visitación de los Yndios Chupachos: Inka et Encomendero 1549," *Travaux de l'Institut Française d'Études Andines* 5 (1955-1956).

4.   The book referred to is Iñigo Ortiz de Zúñiga, *Visita de la Provincia de León de Huánuco en 1562* (t.1 1967, t.2 1972).

five hundred men who are soldiers. Military work and cultivating work were the two things the state expected of more people [than any other kinds of work]. You can do many other things and the list is the kind of list that you would get in a normal human community, important and unimportant, luxury items, ceremonial items, decorative items, the rest does not matter. But that one thousand men, even if many of them are the very same [ones]—you do not have to assume that the five hundred cultivating are different from the five hundred soldiers. We do not know in what way these various categories overlap or how frequently you had to serve. The document doesn't tell us that. But you clearly see the kind of revenues the state had and that it was always in energy, in time, not in goods.

Going with it—and I have no time to develop it, but I would like to mention it at this point—is the fact that at no time do you have anywhere here a standing army. The same principle which governs contributions in energy to produce revenues for the state, namely ethnic groups that take their turns and have a quota, is exactly the [same] principle by which the army was recruited. The local ethnic group under the system of indirect rule that I think we can say they had, would assign certain people to military duty and they fought with their own weapons and under their own ethnic leadership. As you will see in the next and final talk, every one of these categories which I set up as the norm today, I will show tension within it, the difficulties within it, why it cannot really continue working the way it was working at some abstract [date], let us say 1580 [sic].[5] Many things are changing, and the final talk will be primarily devoted to the changes and to seeing in which ways the system I am now describing was suffering serious strains.

The one thing that's important for us before we go on is that if you multiply the list that you have [for the Chupaychu], (and most other groups were much bigger) [by all the other territories in the Inca realm]—if you think that this is a fragment, what you have on this map is not really even half of the territory and the people that the state had incorporated. Vast territories to the south and east, and quite large territories to the north were incorporated into the state. If you multiply [this] kind of list, even if you diminish all quantities to one-tenth of what is listed there, you are still getting enormous amounts of real labor invested on behalf of the state, guided by state functioning, and the results of all this effort are very tangible. They produce actual sandals, actual feathers, actual food, actual salt, actual herds get herded. If you multiply this tiny unit, barely visible on a map this size, by all the other groups that were there, and assuming any kind of collection, any kind of handing in, you are obviously dealing with enormous revenue.

Now what do you do with these revenues? In some ways what this state does with its revenues is very comparable to what other states do, and I will not emphasize the things that you know from your study of other states. Obviously, a great deal of the revenues was redistributed continuously to the army. The seventy-five hundred men that you have on the list, when they were in service ate, and were fed in the army installations all along the major highways and before going into battle. The bureaucracy—we do not really know very much new about the bureaucracy. Nothing new has come up in recent years to make us feel we know anything more, and I will not emphasize it, but obviously, more or fewer bureaucrats, they were there by the thousands and they all had to be fed when in service, and all this produce that the peasants on your list multiplied by a thousand could produce, the bureaucracy ate. The court, the dozens

---

5. This is clearly an error in transcription, since 1580 is post-European invasion, and Murra refers to a time when the Inca Empire was functioning at its fullest, perhaps 1480, before the tensions of which he speaks began. Unfortunately, we do not have the original reel-to-reel tape recording of the third lecture, as we have for the other three. FYW heard that tape many years ago, but somehow it was lost during the intervening years.

and dozens of wives of the king coming from all the different defeated and conquered groups, because he married a woman from every community he had defeated, all those wives, all the children, all the attendants, all the dead bodies. If you notice, the two last kings are dead—yet their mummies have whole series of custodians. So did all the other mummies and other groups provided custodians for all the other mummies. So, living and dead kings must have their retainers and all these people are fed from these revenues.

Finally, the church. There is nothing new on it, and you know the standard clichés, I will not burden you with them, but all these things are functioning, and all those people eat. The revenues are used to maintain them. All of it takes place in what is clearly a redistributive system. The only man who describes it at all says: every fourth day (which is very sensible in the Andes, everything happens in fours), on the fourth day food would be laid out in the public plaza, and the various royal lineages and the various royal houses would come and take their share. We have nothing more detailed, this is a very old description, it might come up later in the discussion today, but it is in a redistributive shape, it is always accompanied by music. It is always accompanied by a festive spirit, the redistribution is pretty much as you have known it in other societies and I have nothing new to say.

I would like to go on and attract your attention to features of this particular system which are less obvious, which cannot be found in all other systems, in all other states of this nature. To do that, I would like to get away from the festive, the mixture of festivity and redistribution at the center, and think of the same redistributing state as an investor, as an organizer of economic activities—of really doing something with what is coming in beyond feeding multiple wives and courtiers and churchmen and the obvious normal things that happen in the capital of a kingdom of this sort. It is this investment aspect, it is this productive economic aspect which I think should not be neglected and this is where we have a little bit of information.

One thing that is important and should not be forgotten is the insistence by the elite that the [Pax Incaica] was really brought into the area. Many other writers who have no reason to defend the Inca rule nevertheless admit that an aspect of the spreading of the rule was the endless warfare that wracked the system before. And you have it very interestingly in the pictures of Guaman Poma.[6] Guaman Poma has a picture showing royal emissaries actually erecting borders [boundary markers].[7] And the erection of these stone indicators of where the boundary lines ended is an important one because you are indicating not only where the various ethnic groups ended—which anybody till today can tell you. An adolescent of fifteen can take you through the whole area of what belongs to [his community], because as he has grown up he has constantly been taken on trips to know, to recognize, to witness the places which his community controls. So this has always been there. But the additional thing that happened at this boundary setting is the fact that this [demarcation of territory], at the same time as it decided limits and where it separated the various ethnic groups, also marked the lands alienated by the crown for crown and state purposes. This also happened at the same time. And you get a sense of that from the constant complaints received by the Spanish authorities later on, in which communities and ethnic groups come to Lima or Cuzco and say we lost out at the time when the Incas set out the boundaries. You see, the setting had taken place so recently before the coming of the Europeans, fifty, sixty, eighty years before,

6.   Felipe Guaman Poma de Ayala, *Nueva Corónica y Buen Gobierno* (Paris: Institut de'Ethnologie, 1936 [1613]).

7.   Guaman Poma (1936 [1613]) provides a number for each of the drawings in his manuscript. Murra refers to drawing number 352 which depicts two royal Inka men, surveyors, building a boundary marker of dressed stone between two adjacent territories.

that the memory of the folk about both the boundaries that were set and what they had lost through alienation was very much alive. And therefore the European documents reflect a particularly European litigation—litigation in European times, not European litigation. Litigation in European times reflects this boundary setting, it was a real *act*. It really did something.

Next, the state organizes production by extending the irrigation network. I am speaking now of the highlands. Archaeologists have told us that the irrigation network on the coast was not expanded in Inca times, but in the highlands there is evidence of the expansion. And not just of irrigation, but particularly of terracing. You can—remember the slides I showed a week ago in which I showed primarily peasant terraces, tiny terraces; a room of this size would have six, seven, eight terraces in it. They are very small and they are built with walls that can be done with peasant energy mobilized locally. State terraces, on the contrary, are monuments, are palaces. The walls—all the stonework in the state terraces is faced stone, the classical kind of Inca architecture you have seen all your life in picture books. But it is used not only for temples, it is used not only for bathhouses, it is used not only for palaces of the king. Over and over again, where you clearly have new [territory] and an effort to expand cultivated territory, the walls supporting the terraces are dressed stone like you would have in a palace or in a temple. And of course, that kind of land must be irrigated, and all of that is clearly new. You do not have an expansion in this situation.

Many of the other things like peasant terraces or peasant irrigation you cannot tell if it is [expansion] or not. In the case of the state terraces it is an unmistakably Cuzco-architectured terrace. Now they have not all been studied adequately yet. They should be studied very well, and it would not be hard because they are centered in certain areas and are rare elsewhere. One could, by just being energetic enough, walking up and down, find vast expanses. We have pictures of many of them. They have never been studied in a serious way. Like, how much land did they cover? What were they cultivated to? What is their relationship to other state installations? All this could really be done quite readily, and I think, will be done in years to come.[8]

Next are roads, the maintenance of roads. I was telling one of my colleagues at dinner how incredulous the local elite, the local middle class today is about the exact nature of these roads. We have read about them all our lives, and yet they are still startled to see how mile after mile after mile of roads, how protected the roads are. Again, how much energy must be mobilized to first build them, and secondly to maintain them under Andean circumstances. And all of this was done, all of this was possible because all this endless revenue pouring into the state's coffers was then in turn redistributed to people, peasants mostly, but for the engineers guiding the work; most of the poor peasants in the particular area in which the work was taking place, they were fed from what was redistributed by the state out of peasant

---

8. There are few archaeological or engineering studies of Inca terraces or of Andean terraces, whether prehistoric or in current, traditional form. Cf. Mayer and Fonseca Martel (1979), Denevan (1987: 255-259; 1995: 21-43), Treacy (1994), Treacy and Denevan (1994: 91-110), Santillana (1999: 61-108), and Valencia Zegarra (2004: 71-82).

In their 1979 ONERN report on agrarian systems in the Cañete drainage, Mayer and Fonseca discuss the impressive kilometers of ancient agricultural terraces, some of which are still in use, on the steep, upper *qiswa* slopes that center on the village of Laraos, (3,660 masl).

"Although we did not always underline the Inca survivals, finding maize terraces in Laraos that have been under continuous cultivation for a millennium certainly played on that note," (E. Mayer, personal communication 2015). "We noted that the hydraulic system practiced by the ancient Peruvians is one of the pillars of communal organization that is still in force in our current communities," (1979: 25). [HL trans.] Section "La Agricultura y Ganadería en la Cuenca de Cañete, 19-34; Subsection "El Regadío y el Cultivo del Maíz. (Mayer and Fonesca 1979: 24-27)

production. We could go on to other public works, but I think the point is made and we do not want to persist.

Let me linger on two other features, which I think are also very Andean and should not be forgotten. The most interesting one is, of course, weaving. I have, in this article I have already mentioned,[9] gone into detail about it, but I think I must bring it up again even though I have published about it because it is such an important aspect of both reciprocity and redistribution. Do not forget that this was the one commodity of the highest value, comparable only to gold in the European world. Not only is it of the highest value, but it is the highest form of art. More, different kinds of textiles were woven, going back, not just in Tawantinsuyu times, but going back two and three thousand years before our era. There is a five thousand year tradition of textile-making as the highest form of art in the Andes, which is in some parts, fully functional today. We could take you to villages where every single woman does works of art in cotton and wool. These are disappearing, and the next generation in these villages will not do it.[10] But it is a fully-functioning tradition, and this is, as the European chroniclers saw it, the very intelligent ones among the Europeans said there is nothing in Christendom like this textile tradition.

No one weave, no one technique, no one fiber. The complex of the energies that went into it, the artistry that inspired it, and most importantly, what people did with the finished goods once they had them. All this is very characteristically Andean and I would go further and say that in no life situation, in no crisis situation, in no moment in your life, in no relationship with anybody else, […] in the very intimate and very reciprocal way, to the kind of balanced reciprocity you get with people you barely know, to political relationships—any kind of interpersonal or intergroup relationship has to be lined with cloth. You have to give it a lining of cloth to relate to particular individuals or to particular groups. You can see it easily in terms of sacrifices. This is what happens, of course, in economies of this kind. You have an awful lot of stuff and one of the things you can do with it is destroy it. So hundreds of pieces of marvelous cloth, which took maybe a year to weave were burned every morning in the sacrifices in the capital. Cloth in vast quantities was burial goods. [William] Duncan Strong, you have probably seen in his reports, he has a report for five hundred yards of cloth, found just lying in the ground.[11] A man buried, an important man, buried with eighty garments, all of them obviously new, never worn. And fortunately on the coast everything is kept so nothing deteriorates, nothing rots away. So we know everything like this.

There is no gift more valuable and there is no status relationship, there is no tense or delicate relationship between two former enemies or two people of a different position in society that will not

9.   John Victor Murra, "Cloth and its Functions in the Inca State," *American Anthropologist* 64(4) (1962a).

10.   Two outstanding, current examples of support and guidance provided by anthropologists to the successful revitalization and management of local, fine textile production and sale, for a national and international market, occur in Bolivia. Antropólogos del Sur Andino (ASUR), based in Sucre and founded in 1986 by Verónica Cereceda and Gabriel Martínez, helped establish and continues to play a central role in the training and production of a textile organization of Jalq'a and Tarabuco, Quechua-speaking women weavers in the high mountain valleys, northern Department of Chuquisaca (cf. Healy 2001). From 2003 to the present, the Instituto de Lengua y Cultura Aymara (ILCA), based in La Paz, continues, similarly, to assist local, indigenous community organizations in the region of Challapata, the south-eastern corner of the Department of Oruro, to organize, manage, and improve the textile production of Aymara-speaking women in all stages of textile technology: from attention to the health of camelid herds that provide the wool for spinning yarn to the sale of the woven webs (cf. Arnold and Espejo 2010).

11.   William Duncan Strong, *Paracas, Nazca, and Tiahuanacoid Relationships in South Coastal Peru* (Salt Lake City: Society for American Archaeology, Memoir 13, 1957).

always be accompanied by offerings of cloth and counter gifts. You constantly contributed and you constantly are giving away garments. Not yards of goods, but ready-made finished garments of many, many different kinds.

What is important for our purposes here today is the political function of cloth redistribution, the giving away of cloth and how it is used politically. I have no time to go into all the other features. Besides, it is all written up. This is most visibly recognizable at the moment of defeat. The defeated conquered group, as it gets incorporated into the state system, is offered, and we do not know quite if it is to every household head, or to every man, woman and child, they say to everybody, but it is not clear to whom, but anyway "everybody," the first thing they get as they are incorporated is a garment. You give them cloth. Those of you who are familiar with what this kind of redistribution means in economies of this kind will readily recognize that we are confronted here with a pump-priming enterprise in which dependency is created. As you give stuff away you obligate the other fellow.

You create a situation in which he owes you something. This is generally presented by the Europeans as an example of generosity, and magnanimity. The Europeans see it, and, particularly apologists for the system, like [Guaman Poma] writing for Europeans, see it as magnanimity—this great marvelous king, who was, as they say in Spanish in that period "*franco y liberal*"—liberal with his things, giving it all away, and *franco*—open, open-handed, in that sense. And of course, you and I, who know systems of this kind, particularly those at work in Africa and elsewhere, which are fully functioning today, know that what is really happening here is that you are creating an obligation. Much more than being *franco* and *liberal*, what you are creating is citizens, you are gaining dependents, you are creating people who will forever after be producing the stuff on that list in front of you. This is how the first step is made. It is started, not by an order, although the order is there implicitly, you start by a gift, you give away that which you value most, and in this system what you value most is cloth.

So what you have then, clearly, from a very early point, and I do not know how far back this goes, but judging from the excellence of textiles, judging by the excessiveness with which a wide variety of textiles are present in so many situations, archaeologically speaking, I would say that this is a very old technique. I do not think this is a new technique. I do not think the peasants were startled when the representative of Tawantinsuyu called them in and said all right fellows, line up. There is a good picture in Livingstone,[12] by the way, showing the Lozi king standing there with a roll of red cloth, he had hundreds of yards of red cloth, and cutting away and giving everybody a hunk in much the same sort of way. I am sure we could find parallels in other arts of the world. But what is happening here is you have reciprocal relationships and particularly this redistributive aspect of them, incorporated into a hierarchical situation. You have a stretching out of what was obviously easy to do within a small kinship community or a small ethnic group like the Chupaychu, stretched out and expanded into the dozens and dozens of ethnic groups that were incorporated into Tawantinsuyu through the years of conquests.

The second, and in a way maybe even more important or just as important as the textile, but very different, that we must understand is peculiarly Andean, is if you ask yourself what do they do with it all. Well, a lot of it they gave away. But there is another important part. Before we give it away you have to

---

12.   We have been unable to locate this particular picture in the Livingstone publications or in other, anthropological publications about the Lozi (FYW and HL). At my request, Perrice Nkombwe, Keeper of Ethnography and Art at the Livingstone Museum, Livingstone, Zambia, reviewed the museum's extensive collection of printed and digitized photographs. She reports that she and her staff did not find the image to which Murra refers (Perrice Nkombwe, personal communication December 2015). I thank Perrice Nkombwe for her care and patience in meeting my request. (HL)

make sure that somehow you will have access to it, that somehow it will keep, that it will not rot away, that the moths will not get into all these lovely woolen goods. And this is what these pictures are all about. One of the things not properly recognized is the fabulous quality of the warehouses. What they did with it all is that first of all they stored it. And in order to have a place to store it you had to build, through this kind of *mit'a* or day labor, you had to build everywhere throughout the kingdom, of stone, above ground, if it's the highlands where it rains, underground on the coast where it never rains, but warehouses, warehouses, warehouses. Thousands of them standing all over the place. This is why when in present times, I submit the thesis, which Mr. Millon has, the thesis of Craig Morris.[13] We are dealing with the warehouses in at least one administrative center; the reaction of the present day agronomists is not "how great that we know about our pasts," what they say is that we need that to go to the minister of agriculture to convince him that storage can be done in this country. Because so frequently all this past accomplishment is thrown out. All this past accomplishment is considered underdevelopment. Like the mother tongue, like the knowledge of verticality, like all the crops, the warehouse system is part of underdevelopment, and therefore rejected. So, I would like you to take a look at some of these warehouses. I have two kinds: a state system and the peasant system.

This is the hill above Huánuco Pampa (Fig. 10) which is not a major provincial capital or administrative center, but it is a very good-sized [administrative center]; you found one of these every five days of walking. You find one system at the end of each day's walk and it will have twenty, twenty-five, thirty warehouses. But this is at the end of each five days. And this hill is full of rows (Fig. 11). There are [almost five hundred] warehouses, much bigger than me, twice as tall as I am and eight, ten, twelve meters wide (Figs. 12, 13). And the [Huánuco Pampa site] map on the board shows you in detail, on this particular hill, every one of those things is a warehouse.[14] So I will pass this around.

The other is what it looks like at the local level. This is a small village. You see the whole village in the picture, with the two kinds of buildings on it. There are houses, which are ordinary kinds of one-story houses, they have a straw roof, and are very much like houses in the area today. What you do not have in the area today are the marvelous storehouses, which are two stories high. They can be easily distinguished in this village, and I will pass this around so you can see it. I have pictures for those who are interested in more detail later on. This is good enough for the moment. The Europeans could not get over these warehouses, and the reaction was much the same as it was to textiles.

This is why I picked these two things. I get the hint about it from the Europeans themselves. They had never seen textile production of this kind, either in quantity or in quality, and they had never seen a warehouse system. As they say, the Christians thought that no matter how much they took, it would never end. And of course they took and took.

---

13. Craig Morris, "Storage in Tawantinsuyu" (PhD diss., University of Chicago, 1967). See also: Craig Morris, "Huánuco Pampa and Tunsukancha: Major and Minor Nodes in the Inka Storage Network" (Norman: University of Oklahoma Press, 1992a) and "The Technology of Highland Inka Food Storage", in *Inka Storage Systems*, ed. Terry Y. Levine (Norman: University of Oklahoma Press, 1992b); János Gyarmati and András Varga, *The Chacaras of War. An Inka State Estate in the Cochabamba Valley, Bolivia.* (Budapest: Museum of Ethnography, 1999).

14. The rows of circular storehouses (*qollqa* in Quechua) which contained capped ceramic jars filled with maize kernels, are situated at the lower altitudes on the hillside that overlooks the city, Huánuco Pampa. The rows of rectangular storehouses, arrayed higher up on the hill slope where the temperatures are lower, held fresh potatoes packed in bales of straw. The maize stored under these conditions could remain fresh for about four years; the potatoes for about one year (cf. Morris 1992).

Figure 10. Site plan by Craig Morris of the Inka administrative city Huánuco Pampa, built on the high puna (over 3,800 masl), Dos de Mayo Province, Department of Huánuco, Peru. The hill overlooking the southernmost zone of the city accommodates close to 500 storehouses (*qollqa*) that supplied city residents with maize and fresh potatoes. Craig Morris, Huánuco Pampa Archive; courtesy of the Division of Anthropology, American Museum of Natural History, New York.

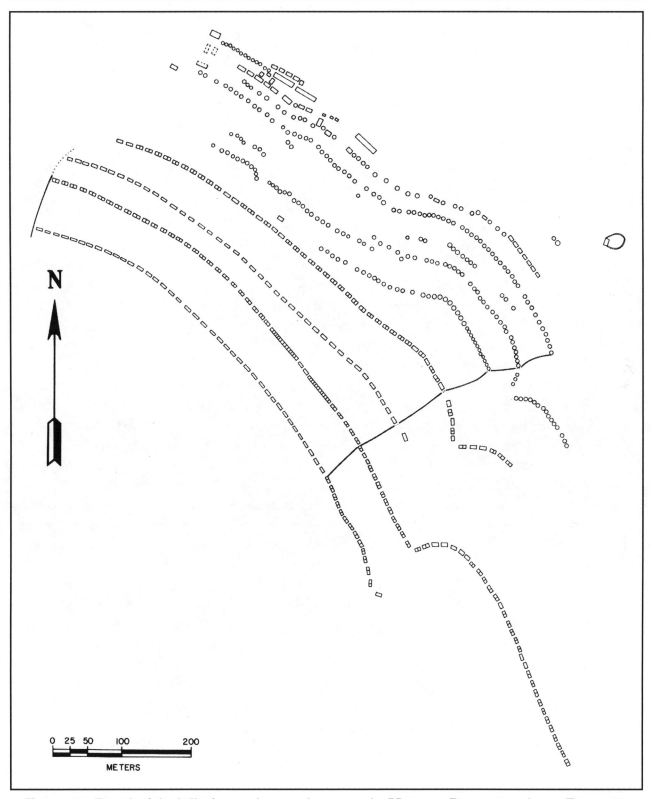

Figure 11. Detail of the hillside storehouses shown on the Huánuco Pampa site plan in Figure 10. The rows of circular *qollqa* at the low altitudes stored maize; the rectangular buildings higher up on the hillside stored fresh potatoes that require colder temperatures to prevent sprouting. Craig Morris, Huánuco Pampa Archive; courtesy of the Division of Anthropology, American Museum of Natural History, New York.

Now, in 1547 [sic, 1549], about the same time as this paper that you have in your hands was drawn up, which was done after the civil war. But during the civil war, two years earlier, in 1547, the king's army is stuck at one point in a rather difficult situation. They have no food, and the quartermaster of the group who later became one of our best students of Andean things, decided to use the old warehouses, this is fifteen years, fifteen, sixteen years after the European invasion, and he goes to the local regional, important, bigger system of warehouses, found a man. "Yes," he says, "of course." He fed the army, he says, for seven weeks. His army was two thousand strong. And they ate seven weeks from the warehouses that the king had in this area [at Xauxa]. As the quartermaster, he got to be friends with the man in charge. He discovered the man had a complete [*quipu*] record of everything the Europeans had stolen from [the Xauxa warehouses], [from] 1532 to 1547.[15] All that, I mean, he was prepared in case the kingdom came back the next day! He had his books, he was all protected, he knew exactly where he could go ... he could say that this was taken .... And what is more, for fifteen years after the coming of the Europeans, people in the area keep producing and feeding into the original warehouse the stuff they had always fed in. So the system continues after 1532. Now we do not know when it stops, and obviously it had different stopping dates in various parts. But in this particular part it goes on for fifteen years and the warehouses are still full, and these men did eat for seven weeks. One of my great aspirations in life is to find the quartermaster's accounts. Because in his story he says, "... and I will not tell you any more because it will bore you." Since I am a man ready to be bored, I hope to find it someday. I have found so many laundry lists, I figure I can get this.

I will finish with these warehouses, because, beyond their size, there are many technical problems which we should not go into, we should not waste time at this moment. I would like to say only one thing that deals with this redistributive quality in all these warehouses. In 1962 I published an article in *American Antiquity*,[16] in which I said what I wanted to do [in fieldwork at Huánuco Pampa] during that three year period [1963-1966]. And one of the things I held out for this city is, I said, look, so many people served in it, they came from so many different places, and if we go and make a survey of the pottery we will be able to discover what the radius of action is, was. How far did they draft the people to come and work in the city? And we spent quite a lot of time looking for it. But I only promised that, of course I cannot deliver, but I only promised that because I did not understand my own system well enough. If my system is right—that you go, and you work, and while you are working, while you are giving of your energy, you are fully supported and the state provides for you through these redistributive mechanisms, out of these warehouses—I should not have expected to find anything. And sure enough, we never found any local pottery—they found two million potsherds [at the Huánuco Pampa site]. There is no pottery that you can identify with any of the villages around and we had the sample of the villages, like the one that is passing around over there, we know what the pottery from that village looks like, and we know those guys work here because it says so. "We go and it takes us two days to get there and we do this kind of work." Yet we cannot prove it archaeologically. Why? Because these people were there, but all the time they were on service, they were fully supported.

The story of the Europeans, when they say, "the king saw a man carrying dirt in his own *manta* and the king ordered that another [state-issued] manta be brought." Well, we treat that as, you know, poetry, we

15.   Murra published the "quartermaster's document," which relates a court case that the Lords of *Hatun* Xauxa brought to a Lima court in 1561. The document records the goods that the Spaniards were given or stole from the imperial Inka storehouses in Xauxa from 1533 to 1548 (Murra 1975b). For Inka imperial quipus, cf. Gary Urton. 2017. Inka History in Knots. Austin: University of Texas Press.

16.   John V. Murra, "An Archaeological "Restudy" of an Andean Ethnohistorical Account," *American Antiquity* 28(1) (1962b).

do not think it is serious. Yet in a way, it is. A man on duty did not bring his coffee cup with him. He was issued a cup and he drank out of a state cup. Now, his wife may have made that state cup or somebody else whose job it was to make cups for the state, because they do this, all the things that I list toward the bottom,[17] say how many people were making pots. Now, his wife may have made that, but she made it according to a state standard. This is the really unbelievable thing, because you have made a model, but you do not really believe in it. It seems so fantastic! It seems so hard to believe that in a very concrete situation it really worked that way, yet it obviously does.

Let me move on. There is a great deal of reciprocal service which involves not only your kinfolk, not only your fellow ethnic group members, but involves authority, kings like the Lupaqa kings, the very big king at the top in Cuzco all benefited from this kind of services. In turn, they distributed among us a wide variety of goods when we were in service. But obviously this model must be inadequate. There must be many a slip-up within the system. Any number of times, people absconded, people did not show up when they were supposed to deliver. Any number of times the system did not fulfill what it promised to fulfill. The warehouse was supposed to be filled, yet it is half empty. Or there is a calamity. In this kind of a system, the state, in its islands of production, gets nothing in the year of drought, or the year of floods, or a year of frosts, or a year of hail. So, the state takes real chances. By not having tribute, it takes real chances that there might be nothing delivered. In that case, we must obviously allow for some kind of exchanges taking place, within the favor of the official system, and within the margins that do not function or do not quite fit, of the ethnic groups and their characteristics.

So we must look at the whole third aspect of this economic life, which are the nature of the exchanges that exist here. Archaeologically speaking, we can show barter relationships of some sort, we do not know what kind, but some kind of exchange is taking place two and three and four thousand years ago. For example, this entire desert coast, in which nothing deteriorates, and if anything has been buried there it lies there forever after in perfect condition, you frequently find in the early strata two- and three- and four thousand years ago, any number of things that come from the Amazon, clearly tropical things that would not live on that desert coast, all kinds of parrots, all kinds of animals. You have on the designs—speaking of pottery, you will get all kinds of Amazonian ideas. Levi-Strauss has pointed out that [depicted on] the pottery in the [South Coast], pottery more than two thousand years old, you get this very common idea, mythological idea from the Amazon today, in which mankind is settled, each ethnic group, at its particular river fork, and you put the people into a snake canoe. You have a snake, which is a canoe, and the canoe is alive being a snake and the people are inside and are being delivered by snake canoe to the place where they will live ever after. You see it represented over and over and over again, on these Nazca pots.

This endless archaeological evidence for connection between the Amazon and the coast [...]. In some of our own work that Collier and I did many years ago in Ecuador,[18] we also showed very much the same. The distances are very great, but the unmistakable connection. Elsewhere, not just in the desert, but the archaeological work of [Luis] Lucho Lumbreras, a Peruvian archaeologist, has shown that in the [*lomas*] areas that occasionally get covered with grass, [not seasonally] but occasionally get covered with grass you immediately have herders from the hills come down and around these grassy areas which last for

---

17. Cf. Footnote 1.

18. Donald Collier and John Victor Murra, *Survey and Excavations in Southern Ecuador.* (Chicago: Field Museum of Natural History Anthropological Series 35, Publication 528, 1943).

some months, trade, barter takes place.[19] Coastal goods are taken up, then and now, and exchanges of a small kind do take place.

What is interesting is the suggestion the archaeologist, the American archaeologist who used to work down in the Andes, called [Louis] Lou [Stumer],[20] he has a suggestion which nobody else has followed up, and it would be interesting to see if other scholars could confirm, that while there are endless examples of forest, Amazon forest—desert coast connections, in the early strata, these get rarer and rarer in later strata. As you begin to get the influence of highland states—what in Andean archaeology are known as horizons—once the horizons begin to hit you very hard, much of this evidence of forest to coast contact begins to disappear. There is much less of it. Now many people do not quite feel that the evidence is all in on this, but we should keep it in mind, particularly as the man I like best among the Europeans[21] clearly says if you talk to the old people, they will tell you that in the old days there was much more commerce than there was today. And then he tells you what the different objects in the trade were. But again, this information is sketchy, this information is [in] passing, and is liable to various interpretations. We are not quite sure what he meant and I am going to leave it.

Another kind of exchange is thoroughly documented. There is no doubt whatever, namely long distance trade, what [Karl Polanyi] calls [administered] trade.[22] Up and down the ocean go balsa wood rafts that can be built only up here [in Ecuador] because there are no [balsa] trees down there, but with the logs collected up here you have balsa ships—balsa rafts—with sails going up and down the coast. The Europeans [who sailed south of the equator for the first time with Pizarro's pilot Bartolomé Ruíz de Estrada] down on Pizarro's second trip[23] briefly describe a very large sailing raft and tell us very clearly what the goods were that they were carrying. Overwhelmingly the raft was filled with tons, literally tons, of [spondylus, *mullu* in Quecha] seashells. Spondylus[24] is a [bivalve mollusk] that does not live in the cold waters of the Peruvian currents but is available up North. And you need this particular shell to make it rain. Throughout the several areas you make it rain by adding powdered shell of this particular kind to your farm when you start [cultivating] at the beginning [of the agricultural year]. You did it then and many people do it today. So there is continuity in this kind of activity. And this is what the raft was bringing back.

---

19.   Lumbreras, Luis G. 1974. *The Peoples and Cultures of Ancient Peru*. Trans. Betty J. Meggers. Washington, D.C.: Smithsonian Institution Press. In 1969 Lumbreras published the original Spanish language book, *De los Pueblos, las Culturas y las Artes del Antiguo Perú*. Lima: Francisco Moncloa Editores. The book was translated and published in English in 1974. Cf. Lumbreras. 1967. La Alimentación Vegetal en los Orígenes de la Civilización Andina. *Perú Indígena*, 11(26) 254-273.

20.   Louis M. Stumer, "Contactos Foráneos en la Arquitectura de la Costa Central," *Revista del Museo Nacional* (Lima) 27 (1958).

21.   Murra likely refers to Polo de Ondegardo whom he considered a reliable sixteenth century Spanish commentator on the Andean society he witnessed and documented only thirty years after the European invasion. A passage in which Polo remarks on memories of "the elders" with respect to the extent of barter and exchanges of goods before and at the time of the Inka appears in Juan Polo de Ondegardo, "Informe al Licenciado Briviesca de Muñatones [...]" (1940 [1561]).

22.   Karl Polanyi, Conrad M. Arensberg, and Harry W. Pearson, *Trade and Markets in the Early Empires* (Glencoe, Illinois: The Free Press, 1957).

23.   In 1526, Ruíz and his crew captured a seagoing balsa raft, with crescent-rigged cotton sails, as it sailed northward along the Ecuadorian coast. On board were twenty men and several tons of cargo, including many silver objects and metal tiaras, crowns, bands, tweezers, dyed clothing with embroidery, emeralds ... and much more. "...Todo esto traían para rescatar unas conchas de pescado": [all this they brought to exchange for some sea shells] (Sámano-Xerez (1937 [1534]: 63-68). Cf. Estete (1918 [1535]); Dewan and Hosler (2008).

24.   *Spondylus princeps*, otherwise known as the "thorny oyster", is found in the warm waters along the Pacific coast at latitudes from the Ecuator north, to the west coast of Mexico and beyond.

What it was taking, you can predict again. In an area without llamas what you are taking is wool goods, clothing and certain kinds of black pots. What else the vessel may have been taking of course, we do not know and unfortunately this is the only description of such a vessel, but in December 1968, a Peruvian colleague of ours [María Rostworowski[25]] found in the national library in Madrid a description of the balsas coming, not where the first man saw it, which was way up here [near Tumbes], but all the way down to here [the Chincha Valley]. Flotillas of sailed rafts were coming down and as soon as this manuscript is widely available you will be able to see it yourselves, we have predicted this all along, and now we have the information. There is long distance administered trade. In the case of the coast up here there may be an earlier and coexisting local trade, which has nothing to do with the Incas, but which is a local activity of these fellows, they do it today, they did it in the eighteenth and seventeenth centuries, and it is a separate story which we do not have to worry about [here].

Now, within this framework comes the title of this talk. What about marketplaces? What about trade? What about commerce, what about exchanges of a different kind, which are not a matter of just occasional things taking place within the chinks of the system, or long distance administered trade by the state. What about exchange of goods within this larger system? And the debate is an interesting one and is just beginning. It is going to get hotter as the years go by. Those of you who are interested in following through, the second name on that left side of the board is a thesis by Dr. Roswith Hartmann[26] at the University of Bonn which deals with markets and in a way, it is by reading her report that I got this title, which really should be in quotation marks [The Inca attempt to "destroy the markets"]. It is not that the Inca state abolishes markets, it is that the students of the Inca state are intent upon making markets appear where I think one would have a hard time finding them. But I think you should look at it, it is a very interesting thesis, afterward. I will give you the reference if you are really interested.

So, the disagreements and the debates have begun and will continue. They are over simple things: how much exchange, of different kinds, beyond the ones I have mentioned, was really taking place? What kind of exchanges were there? Do not forget that this is very complicated country, there are many regional differences. I would not be surprised if a certain kind of exchange took place on the north coast and you would find it nowhere else. I would not be surprised that around Lake Titicaca you would find another kind of exchanges that you would not find anyplace else. All kinds of regional manifestations will be revealed in years to come as people seriously get to work on all these problems.

But I would argue the following: that given the importance of verticality, this access to as many vertical zones of ecology as possible, which I outlined to you in the first lecture, given the importance of reciprocity and redistribution as I talked about them in the second lecture and now. I would expect that the exchanges in Bohannon and Dalton's classification[27] to be only "peripheral." The list of their exchanges changed with particular economic circumstances. If your idea of verticality failed, or for some reason of calamity could not be undertaken, was not functional in any given year or in any given decade, all kinds of barter systems would emerge to replace that which you would normally get through reciprocity. By peripheral they mean, and I mean, that if this disappeared it would be uncomfortable. You might miss out on certain things you depended on getting this particular way, but the basic, the heart of the system would not be affected. And what's more, I do not see where, within the system as described, of

25.   María Rostworowski de Diez Canseco, "Mercaderes del Valle de Chincha en la Época Prehispánica: Un Documento y Unos Comentarios," *Revista Española de Antropología Americana* 5 (1970).

26.   Roswith Hartmann, "Maerkte im Alten Peru" (PhD diss., Universitaet zu Bonn, 1968).

27.   Paul J. Bohannon and George Dalton, *Markets in Africa*, eds. (Evanston, Illinois: Northwestern University Press, 1962).

these ethnic groups producing as much as they could for themselves and never giving up what they had produced for themselves, but owing all these services which are on this list you have, even if it was only one-tenth of what they claimed they handed over. Suppose they only gave one-tenth in any given year, still, this is a fabulous amount of time devoted to producing things that the state needed. Within this kind of system, production for the market, any kind of production for the market, is essentially out of the question. But since this is only logic, and with human affairs logic is not the best counselor, let me give you the few cases that I have of actual, real marketplaces.

I go back to my friends the Chupaychu who have helped me most. The Chupaychu do say in answer to one of the questions, which is "Who are your neighbors and what are your trading relations with them?" This is of course, a questionnaire made in 1559 and you would not get this kind of a leading question today, but still, it is interesting to know the question they are answering. And they begin to list who their neighbors are, and we know who their neighbors are, and then they list what it is that was exchanged within the system. And it is just as interesting to see what they say they exchanged, as to note what they do not say. And since it is not one witness testifying, this is about thirty different communities, as the inspector comes to the village, he reads off the questionnaire—I would have loved to have seen it—particularly if you know how questionnaires are drawn up today and how answers are beaten out of Andean populations today. It would have been interesting to see how they were answering before they had been so traumatized by four hundred years of European persistence. So then you have the question, and the man reads, and the guy answers, "Our neighbors are so and so and so and so, we trade with them." And if it is a lowland guy, he recites his home list, and his list is maize, cotton, feathers, coca leaf, and one more thing. It is very interesting, when they recite the list, community after community, the list is always the same. There is a hierarchy, there are occasional changes in the list, and Robert Bird,[28] our botanist, is convinced that what they are doing is the reading [of] a quipu, the reading of knots, because they are always saying, reciprocating with a canned answer to the questionnaire. Partly you can say this is a canned answer, because, they have all learned it, but it is very interesting to see how [the people in] these various communities who had not heard the answer of the other guys, at least not as witnesses, what their answers are.

The highland fellows are giving wool, dried meat, occasionally fish, because way, way up you have little lakes that have tiny fish that are [caught and] dried as kind of a [relish or garnish]. You just eat them separately, like, let us say smelts or, better than smelts, what do you call that? Whitebait, some of the lakes up in [the Great Lakes area] used to produce them before pollution. So, again, the list from above is one thing and the list from below is another thing, but it is always the same. [No staple] food. Note what is missing in both lists. Food is missing in both lists. No list contains food. None of the tubers that form the staple food are ever listed on any list. I think this is very interesting. Secondly, the thing that you would expect because it is of high value and everybody loves it and everybody wants more of it and people are hoarding it and people are dying wrapped in it: cloth. No cloth.

So what is missing is the most obvious things—the staple food, and what is missing is the most valuable thing, namely, cloth. What you have is an intermediary area of things which are not staple food, but are nice: dried fish, dried meat from the sierra, peppers, maize from below—maize is not a staple, you

---

28.   Robert Bird was a member of John Murra's field research team at Huánuco Pampa. Bird, an ethnobotanist, not only studied the botanical materials and floral environments pertinent to the project, he also drew up a detailed map that locates the ethnic groups, *mitimae*s, and many of the villages Iñigo Ortiz de Zúñiga visited and reported on in 1562. Murra published the map in Volume 1 of the Huánuco *Visita*; (1967); a color-coded version of the map appears here in Figure 6.

use it to make beer, but you might for eating—it is good. You can obviously live without it, but it is nice to have it. And this is what goes back and forth. Not staples, not the truly valuable things, but the thing sort of in between that is very nice and very good to have. This is the only actual marketing situation. I do not even know if there was a marketplace. They referred to one spot where this took place. A place in Chinchaycocha [Chincha cocha: Lake Junín]. It is a very large lake, not quite as large as Titicaca, but it is the largest lake in the whole central Andes, very high—four thousand meters, and the only people there today are the US metal miners. They are there in the communities they built up—otherwise in the old days what there were, were herds. It is really—only some of the very bitterest and most durable [varieties] of potatoes would grow, and other tubers like [oca, ulluco] which we do not even know in this country. So there is little agriculture, primarily herding, but around that lake for some reason is where the exchanges took place.

I suggested in that same *American Antiquity* article[29] that it would be nice to find this place [on the borders of Lake Junín] again, for the very same reasons that I wanted to excavate in the administrative center, because I kept hoping that somehow I would get the radius of action: How far did these provincial centers reach out? How cohesive is this particular state structure? An archaeological guy could reach it, I could convince an archaeologist to spend the necessary six or eight months under these conditions of four thousand meters of altitude—it is forty-one hundred meters up in the air. It is really an impossible place, it took fully two years of working in this area and in one way I found myself perfectly at home, I was discussing problems at the local university, because these are these mining towns and they are very eager to have universities going in them. So, I did not even notice I was up there. I really felt that finally after two years I had acclimated to these particular circumstances.

Dr. Hartmann has said that the hope of finding such a market is fantasy. She does not think that we can do it. I think we can. I think it will take a real survey, really hard work, but the market, the marketplace would be worth finding, even if it was not a very elaborate thing. But if they have come for a very long time, and think this is what I am betting on, I am betting on Andean continuity. That if they did it one place, just like the Japanese found shrines reaching over fifteen hundred years because they kept going back and back and back to the shrine, if marketing activity was at all important, and the way they describe it at the margin of this lake, I would expect to find something enduring, not elegant, maybe, no palaces, no guards' booths in which the Inca guards are watching over it, but simply the deposits, because a market produces an enormous amount of debris, all the broken potsherds, all the bones, all the stuff that a market routinely produces in just ... even if you hold it only once a year, but you do it over five hundred years, I would expect to find something quite interesting. And if it is a fantasy, I think it is a [possible] fantasy.

I have only one more example of a marketplace, an alleged marketplace which I mentioned in passing earlier today, and that is the marketplace in Cuzco proper, you see, at the other end of the system. This Chupaychu system is probably one of the smallest groups in the whole Andes, a tiny enclave that we happened to get a glimpse of through the papers I managed to get. But look at the other end. We have descriptions by several Europeans of quite large marketplaces in Cuzco. But since they are not detailed, since you do not know who is there, it is not like the kind of descriptions you get in Mesoamerica where they tell you what was actually there. This was just the activities going on. What is perfectly possible from the description is another interpretation, namely that what you are having there—you are witnessing the redistributive act. All the thousands of royals that hang around the capital, all the people at court, all the

---

29. Cf. Footnote 15.

priests got fed every fourth day, we know that. Yet it must take some kind of expressive form. It must occur somewhere, in some plaza in some way. This is what the Europeans witnessed.

I do not know that this is what happened, but it is just as possible that this is what was happening, and certainly what we need is more research, more excavation, to settle and see how important marketing activities were. Notice another thing about it all: with the exception of the long-distance people who must have accompanied these rafts, nobody pretends that there were any traders. On the contrary, even people who say there were markets, say over and over that there are no traders. And they say to you, "There are not traders like you have. We have no wholesalers," they say. "We have no [commerce]." Even Garcilaso himself who does not miss an opportunity to exalt his mother's ancestors' accomplishment, says, "Well, what they did is they sat in the market and bartered back and forth, with the little bit they might have."[30]

There is clearly no evidence for all-purpose money and barely any evidence for special purpose money. Some of the highly-valued things like maize appear in exchanges. But there is no evidence really, beyond maize—and coca leaf, too, sometimes shows up in exchanges. As I have done all along in these talks, I want to emphasize a feature of Andean research which makes it possible, which even I was not aware of fifteen years ago, namely, how much continuity is present today and how you can use modern ethnological work to test some of your hypotheses about the past.[31] It is very important to see how many money-less market places are functioning today.

Right outside Cuzco there is one to which I have been several times. It is a place called Chincheros, not to be confused with Chinchaycocha, which is the lake on which there is some evidence [of market activity]. Chincheros is a town in which every blessed Sunday there are several hundred people from all over that area coming and exchanging, bartering, always without using any money. These are people who on Saturday were downtown in Cuzco buying yards of plastic sheeting to be used as raincoats, transistor radios, these are people thoroughly aware of the marketing system. They know all about it, they know its rules. In their own market—which as recently as 1963, which is the last time I was there, though it may have stopped since '63, but in '63—it was a fully functioning enterprise. All transactions, but for one US psychoanalyst who browbeat a woman into selling him—for money—her shawl, which was really very beautiful and I was so ashamed because I took this idiot to the place, but he essentially kept offering more money, since there was no limit to the money he was ready to pay and there was a point at which she decided she should not avoid this opportunity.

---

30. This is likely the passage from Garcilaso that Murra mentions: "Tampoco se daban ni arrendados porque ni supieron arrendar ni comprar ni vender, porque no tuvieron moneda; trocaban unas cosas por otras, esto es, las cosas del comer y no más. Que no vendían los vestidos ni las casas de las heredades." Garcilaso de la Vega, Inca. 1991 [1609]. Comentarios Reales de los Incas, edited by Carlos Araníbar. Vol. 1, México DF: Fondo de Cultura Económica, p. 345. I thank Frank Salomon for locating this text. HL

31. César Fonseca argues that, whereas in a society in which each human group attempts to achieve self-sufficiency through direct access to diverse microenvironments and ecologies (the vertical archipelago structure), among contemporary highland Andean communities barter often coexists with direct access as a means of achieving self-sufficiency. Fonseca presents ethnographic data from his field research of contemporary communities, many of which Iñigo Ortiz de Zúñiga visited in 1562. In 1562, these communities (such as Tangor, Paucar, Yacán) represented Yacha ethnic groups located along the Río Chaupiwaranga, from the puna to the qiswa zone and included high puna herding villages such as Cauri, at the northwest limits of Yacha territory (Fig. 6 in this volume reproduces a map drawn to locate the sites Iñigo Ortiz visited; the sites Fonseca studied appear on the map).

Fonseca describes the barter arrangements between puna and qiswa dwellers that existed when he carried out his fieldwork (1964-1965). Puna products, derived from herding camelids and sheep (wool, lamb/mutton, leather, ch'arki, ch'uñu, cheese), were exchanged for qiswa products (maize, trigo and other grains, beans, squash). Fonseca (1972a, 1972b: 315-38).

But with the exception of that transaction, I have spent frequently as many as six hours in the market. I have never studied it, so I have never spent the time you have to: you have to go there the night before, you have to see people arriving and you have to stay until afterward. But I have seen this market at different times of year and it works fifty-two Sundays a year. There are similar marketplaces in other parts of the country but Chincheros and Chinchaycocha are simply two places and they are far apart. Chincheros is just outside Cuzco and is way down here almost close to Chile. There are other things that I have heard about, but these two I have actually seen.

Not only that you have several different places up and down through the country. Again I have not made an inventory of these. These are things that turn up as you absorb information. In many places where the national currency exists, and is known and actually used in transaction, but not as money. This is done, again, by people who work in modern, US mines, who belong to trade unions, who appear on radio programs, who have an orchestra which truly includes a harp, panpipes, and a saxophone. These are modern men! Yet, when it comes to trading among themselves, they use national currency, not as money; they use national currency as a standard. For example, there is an inscription on a wall on the [island of Taquile] in the middle of Lake Titicaca. They grow maize, which is incredible, at almost four thousand meters maize appears. The corn cob is the size of half of your thumb, the first phalange of your thumb. People come from hundreds of miles away at harvest time, to get some of this corn. They pay for it, not in money, they pay for it in goods. But both sides use national currency as a standard, at prices which are ridiculous, pennies for a sack. But of course you and I cannot buy it for that price, and they will not give it for money, they will give it only for other equally traditional commodities, parts of the verticality they have lost to Europeans, and which they continue to yearn for, and they exchange.

But everything is phrased not in terms of barter, everything is phrased in money terms that are completely meaningless in terms of the present value of the currency. So money is used as a standard but it is not the means of exchange. You cannot buy anything for money. Money is simply an intermediary within the barter situation. I would say to you that this kind of continuity is not only interesting, it tells you something about the economy of the Andes today, but this is only a part of an approach to commercial transactions to a market system which is very old in this area. In any case, whichever way you look at it, even suppose you refuse to see continuity, suppose you think that much more about this continuity would have to be verified with historical papers which we do not have. What is very clear is that in the old days, a long distance, administered trade coexisted with peripheral exchanges. There was no market system. Marketplaces, if they existed, did not create any kind of linking market system. There was no production for the market.

But one more thing that we must look at, and that is that the oldest African research has given us certain hints about what happens when there is money and when there is no money in the different kinds of market places, and one thing is very clear. When you have the kind of utter absence of money as apparently was the case here, this indicates the possibility that we are confronted here with several different transactional spheres, several different sets of economic exchanges which take place one within the other and which are not necessarily linked. Conversion from one to the other is not necessarily possible. Now, I do not know if this is so or not, but since we have this hypothesis I thought that what we can do with the information I gave you earlier about the market in Chinchaycocha, let us look what we get. Food does not appear in the exchanges as listed. I would then think that food is part of general reciprocity. It is part of things that are normally exchanged within the kinship system, within the reciprocity of people working for each other, or the feeding people with whom you are hospitable, of simply taking care of your normal household duties. Luxuries, if you think that coca leaf, maize and wool and dried meat are luxuries, things which you can get along without, but do like and enjoy and are normally available to ordinary people, if they make an effort, if they control verticality, or if verticality is unavailable, then through barter or peripheral exchanges, some form of exchange. This would be the peripheral exchanges I was telling you about.

The absence of cloth is interesting, you see, that fact that cloth was not bartered, the fact that so much cloth had to be woven for the state. The state always put the fibers, and the local authorities who want things woven always must put the fibers. You will see in the next lecture what happens to it once the state really gets interested and this traditional system no longer produces enough cloth or as much as the state thinks it ought to have. This is where it is interesting, because I think that cloth would fit into the redistributional thing. Cloth would be, then, economically speaking, within another sphere of economic activity. Caught up in the hierarchical redistributive thing which we really know about, but define differently, placed in a different economic sphere from the luxuries of maize and coca leaves and so on.

Now I cannot prove this. I think it would be worthwhile just keeping this in mind as research develops. For example, one obvious thing, we know that cloth appeared in every moment of initiation, for example. At every life crisis from birth to death, cloth was exchanged, cloth was given, cloth was received. We do know that there was bride wealth in the Andes. You see, marriage is so completely obfuscated, so completely invisible because of the stuff about how the king grouped the young people in the row and married them off. Now we know this is nonsense, and we are not beginning to find out what marriage really was like, and we know there was bride wealth, and we know there was sister exchanges, but we do not know yet enough. Even at the local level the mythology is so strong. Obviously something was taking place and we must get into it and really clean it up and see what was really going on. But the appearance of cloth as bride wealth would be a very interesting thing in the definition of the several spheres that I was mentioning before.

As usual, I am caught with a whole page of things that I wanted to tell you about, but the time is up. I will maybe have a chance to incorporate into the final talk where I will try to show how all the things I have said up to now really did not work and how the state was undermining the system that it had inherited and which was working. But I think that it is enough to say that what my feeling is about redistribution and commercial activity is that you do have peripheral exchange; clearly some kinds of exchanges do take place along with redistribution and reciprocity. All three of them are simply aspects of the same kind of economic activity. There is an important thing, which is this long distance administered trade which is just beginning to come in, and which I think, again, we can reach both through archaeology and through the means of documentary sources.

Structural Changes in *Tawantinsuyu* Prior to the European Invasion

In the previous three sessions, I have examined some enduring, long-lasting features of Andean life. I emphasized the effort towards vertical control. I worried about the strength of reciprocal ties and their ability to be stretched to encompass superordinate authorities, to encompass societies which were stratified and complex. I was concerned [in the third lecture] with the redistributive role of the state, not only of some of the local, larger political units invaded by the Incas and incorporated into the Tawantinsuyu, but also with the redistributive role of the crown, of the Cuzco authorities. And [in the third lecture] I also dealt with the marginality of market exchanges.

Now, the picture which emerges from all this work done is obviously incomplete. Your questions have frequently remained without answer, either because I don't know the answer or because I don't yet understand how to put together the separate facts that are available. I suppose the latter is even more frequent than the first. Now, although this analysis is so incomplete, there are certain things that one can say about it and one should keep in mind even though I don't develop them. And it seemed to me that maybe I should restate them, although I have been dropping hints [...] all along.

One is that this is certainly not the first state in the Andes. I constantly talk as if we're confronted for the first time with a very large unit of this kind. If we look at the archaeological material this is clearly not so. Archaeology tells us that previously, centuries before, very large parts of the Andes were incorporated into some kind of unit. Now we can quarrel and discuss what kind of a unit, but it doesn't matter for our purposes at this point. We are confronted here, nevertheless—although it is not the first state—with a very large one, with a very extensive one, probably more extensive than any other, earlier state. So you have certain kinds of problems which are new. If you think back, all the way to the Colombian border [with Ecuador], and all the way south to Jujuy [Northwest Argentina] and all the way south to the Río Maule [about 2 degrees south of Santiago de Chile]. This is a fabulous distance if you remember particularly the nature of the terrain. To keep it all together, to somehow bring cohesion, no matter how limited, no matter how bureaucratic, no matter how thin this cohesion was, nevertheless there is some kind of statecraft needed here to keep it together.

And a final point. Within this overall unit you have a great deal of local varieties. Some are obvious. The variety between the north coast kingdoms, the hydraulic kingdoms of the north coast, and some of the kingdoms of the *altiplano* you can predict without knowing anything about them—that there will be features of social, political, economic organization which will be vastly different. Despite the differences, they somehow were kept together. And a final point, that expansion was so very, very rapid. I don't know how many of you have had a chance to see the criticism of our position that the expansion was so rapid, by a Swedish scholar, Åke Wedin. Wedin published a report[1] recently in which he said it is impossible, with the chronology that Rowe suggests,[2] that the whole of Tawantinsuyu was put together in less than a century, let's say one century in round figures. He, Wedin, thinks it is impossible. And it does seem strange unless you begin to think of some other states of this kind which sometimes are put together over very large surfaces in relatively short time. The question always is how long can we keep it together, and I will not try to deal with it here. But all these features are important as I go into this final session because we must remember them—and everything I say, in a way is modified by the speed, by the size, by the variety within the size.

Now in addition to the problem of political control, where if we were doing a real good job, often we would have to deal with the roads, and I haven't done that. It was a very important network of roads. I hear from Victor von Hagen that he really finally will get back to his Andean materials. He's published only a very popular book,[3] but he does have two years' worth of fieldwork on the roads. And politically, the political function of the roads, of quick communications in such a broken terrain, is a very interesting feature, and the only man that has any serious data on it is von Hagen.[4] He's been working on Roman roads the last decade, but he promises me that as soon as the Roman report is out he will return to write up his Andean theory. I haven't dealt with this in proper detail, but again, it's something to think about, the function of the road.

And I haven't dealt with another topic which I think is important, namely, rebellions: the continuous rebellions which occurred in the one century that this kingdom was spreading and which the European sources manage to report on. So, it's in front of all these phenomena that some kind of cohesion, some kind of political control, existed.

If we move to economic things, the kind of things I've been emphasizing in this series, here again, there is obvious strain put upon the reciprocal redistribution ties between the various groups, and how they were connected to the Cuzco realm. The exploitative needs of the state are obviously constantly growing as the kingdom is growing, as it is spreading to brand new territories, meeting completely new problems, having to keep armies in the field, just a very long time that armies must be kept in the field to reach into central Chile or to reach into the province of Salta, or to reach into northernmost Ecuador. The problems involved economically—never mind the political control, the recruitment, and the maintenance of those troops. But economic support for these troops presents a whole series of problems which

1. Åke Wedin, *La Cronología de la Historia Incaica* (Gotemburgo-Suecia-Madrid: Instituto Ibero-Americano, 1963).

2. John Howland Rowe, "Inca Culture at the Time of the Spanish Conquest," in *Handbook of South American Indians*, Vol. 2. *The Andean Civilizations*, ed. Julian H. Steward (New York: Cooper Square Publishers, 1946).

3. Victor W. von Hagen, *The Desert Kingdoms of Peru* (London: Weidenfeld and Nicolson, 1964).

4. There was no thorough, documented field survey of the Inka road system until John Hyslop's 1984 major work, *The Inka Road System* (New York: Academic Press). Hyslop's study was inspired by John Murra.

constantly increase the needs of the state. The demands made by the state upon the services, the *mit'a* services of the peasantry, obviously are growing all the time.

It is in the light of all these preceding statements that I now turn to what is today's topic, namely: the structural changes, the inevitable structural changes which the people running the state have to think about and the phenomena which take place if they thought about it or not.

Well, the changes that you expect are really visible. Some of them are clearly reported by the early European eyewitnesses. And the obvious first one is, how do you increase revenues? If you are concerned with the growing bureaucracy, a growing court, a growing army, a larger and larger and larger state apparatus, how do you increase your revenues if revenues are limited by whatever can be grown on state islands dispersed through the territory and worked by a peasantry, but which inevitably, under Andean conditions, frequently produced nothing or produced very little? If you don't have tribute, it is the state that is taking the risk. In the case of tribute you can increase or lower the tribute demand, but if you take all the risk by having at your disposal only what can be grown on your own terraces, on your own agricultural land, the risk is complete. In bad years and through much of the Andes, particularly in the south, two years in five the harvest is completely lost. Now in such circumstances, how you increase your revenues becomes a very serious thing, and it is not a matter of squeezing just a little bit. It's a matter of how do the revenues come out.

A factor I cannot evaluate, but I'm sure I just intuit is important, is the frequency of war. Those of you who are familiar with the annual war that the Dahomean kingdom conducted: every blessed year there had to be war. Although it created very many problems on the resources, on the army, on the personnel involved. I don't know how frequently wars were fought [by the Inca state], and since the army is not a standing army, since the army is a peasant army which must return to plant, therefore the length of the annual war or cyclical war is short. You probably remember in the case of the Rwanda, in the oral tradition of the Rwandese dynasty, there are kings who are known as peaceful, and then there are kings who are known or expected to be warlike. You don't have quite this neat a pattern in the oral tradition that the Andean peoples delivered to the Europeans. On the contrary, you get more this Dahomean feeling, that everybody, or almost everybody had a campaign on at all times. These campaigns must be financed. Those camp soldiers must be fed. Those soldiers must be provided with shirts. We have stories about what happens when soldiers do not get what they should get. And you can predict what they should get. They should get cloth. And they should get maize for beer. The same pattern of redistribution which local dukes, local barons get when they visit Cuzco is extended to cover the whole army, and the army had fifteen, twenty, thirty thousand people at any given moment out in the field. The feeding of thirty thousand people—those of you who have been in the army and have contemplated such problems can visualize what it would really mean in this kind of a society. The needs are growing all the time.

Now, on the list of services which I distributed to you [at the last lecture]—the Chupaychu list of services. There are very many kinds of chores, many kinds of energies that the peasantry owes to the state. Some of them are obvious ones and need no elaboration. Some are consequences of verticality. If you have this broken terrain and you have colonies in every level and every ecology, some of this specialization is related to the ecology, namely herders in the high *puna*, salt winners up in the uppermost lakes, because that's where the salt is most frequently found; other people down below, growing coca leaf, producing peppers, getting honey. All those fellows are clearly ecology connected, and we don't have to worry at this point how many of them there were, how hard they worked, how they were maintained. On the whole, they fitted within the reciprocal system of ethnic groups and villages. But there are other crafts which are less ecologically rooted. They don't depend so much on ecology. In the Lupaqa situation, silversmiths and artists are listed. They, of course, can practice their art at any latitude and more important than that, you have silversmiths brought from the coastal kingdoms to Cuzco and clearly still there even ten and fifteen years after the European invasion. All these people are fed from state or royal warehouses and for them, too, production must be continuously increased because the need for jewelry, the need for coca leaf, is an eternal one. It does not really go down; on the contrary, it expands all the time.

But really, I want to talk about quite different things because they are again, as [in the third lecture], specifically Andean. There are problems with increasing revenues in goods which [one doesn't] necessarily find in other parts of the world. And how you increase revenues in these Andean things is maybe where we will get hints to how the system is working.

Let me start, as I did in the last lecture, with textiles. There is no end to the textile needs of the state. Not just the ones I mentioned last time, namely the sacrificial, the burning of cloth daily at the state churches. But there is much more involved here. We have obviously massive production of textiles to be given away to soldiers, since the soldier is paid in cloth. He is rewarded for his services in cloth, and will protest if he doesn't get what he expects. But since textiles are so highly valued in this culture, then you have the whole problem of dexterity, you have the whole problem of specialization of labor, and judging by the artifacts themselves, one could easily predict that as early as 2000 BC, some of the textiles are woven by specialists. You cannot examine the things the Textile Museum in Washington has from the Andes, or what Junius Bird[5] has at the American Museum of Natural History, without being thoroughly convinced that this is not the kind of domestic household production that a woman can weave in between her other household chores. There are too many parts, there is too much fine thread, there is too much care that goes into making of these textiles to even assume the possibility of its being household production. This is clearly the work of artisans.

Now, what happens to these artisans as this production must go up? Under normal conditions every household produced one garment a year with state fiber. But this is not enough. If every soldier must get two garments, yet his wife has produced only one, you can see how as the army grows the demand is bigger, and of course the soldiers [require] only a small part of the number of garments needed. Many of the weavers are men. This is one way that you can increase production, if you could get men to devote full time, instead of a woman devoting part of her household time to weaving. But when the needs grow as fabulous as they seem to have been, because the descriptions of these immense warehouses full to the rafters with bundles and bundles and bundles of cloth, at some point obviously what mit'a can produce is inadequate and some other way has to be found to produce cloth for the new requirements, for the new needs.

And what actually happens is that at some point, and we don't know when, a corps of full-time weavers is set up. These are not peasants on corvée. These are not people in the villages who either weave full-time or part-time but are kept in the context of their ethnic, kinship and other traditional ties. These are corps of professional weavers. We can get some of the insight into what this corps was like by noting that neither the Chupaychu nor the Lupaqa—these two other points in the continuum that I have been playing with ever since we first met [in the first lecture]—they didn't have, there is no evidence, at least, that there was anything like a corps of full-time weavers. Some people are better weavers than others. Some

5. Junius B. Bird was Curator of South American Archaeology at the American Museum of Natural History, New York, from 1931 until 1973. He was a scholar of Andean textiles, especially of the technologies by which textiles were made, in both prehistory and in the present. In 1973 and 1984 the Textile Museum in Washington, DC held the Junius B. Bird Conference on Andean Textiles, in his honor. The presentations at those conferences were published (cf. A.P. Rowe, Benson, and Schaffer (1979), A.P. Rowe (1986)).

are known to produce a finer garment. But the notion of full-time devotion is simply nonexistent in these earlier weavers. Now this does not mean that the Incas necessarily were the very first to set it up. But we meet it only in the Inca context. What is interesting is the name of the people involved. And I put on the board the verb from which the name of the group eventually is derived. *Acllay* is to select, is to pick. The people have been selected for this particular job, and once you take out the verb and make a plural noun of it: *acllakuna*. The weavers, who in this case are all women, are plucked out, selected, chosen, because not everybody can do this job. The job is defined as a[n] honor, as a status thing. For status purposes you are creamed off, away from your community and put on a full lifetime period of weaving chores.

When this happened, we don't know. But it would not surprise me that it is quite late. It is not Incaic and certainly not long before that. The need for cloth goes way up. And these women, just like the women in the Dahomean conditions, where you will remember women formed the beginning of a standing army, the only professional soldiers, the only soldiers who fought year round were women. And all the bookkeeping of the Dahomean kingdom was kept by women. In much the same way these women are taken out of the system, out of their normal kinship ties, deprived of their motherly and wifely roles, and put on a full-time basis for state purposes.

Now, the Europeans see them, not of course, as weavers. The Europeans do not share the enthusiasm for weaving of the Andean peoples, and of course the comparison with nuns to a Mediterranean European in 1532—you can imagine that you don't get as much information on their functions as you might. But most of them, this is what they did. This does not mean that they didn't do other things. And interestingly enough, some of our Andean sources, among those who write, even [record that the aclla] have a status hierarchy. Guaman Poma[6] thinks there were six kinds. Salcamaygua,[7] who is another Andean writer late in the sixteenth century or early in the seventeenth, lists four different kinds. Their functions were more numerous. They served temples, they were part of the court, they obviously had— particularly according to status—they had many other functions. I have picked out weaving, because, again, I am not doing a systematic, thorough coverage of everything, but it is my impression that the decisive factor here which changed their status, which plucked them out from their normal condition and put them to state service, was the endless, infinite demand for more and more cloth.

Let me give one other such similar category and I will then talk about these two groups together in a more structural way. We've noted that the armies fitted into this pattern of reciprocity and redistribution. In the sense that the soldier owed military services in between agricultural duties, he fought with his own weapons under his own ethnic leadership. So if you had fellows who normally fought with slings, they would bring their slings and would be led by a man who understood about deploying troops with slings. Others fought with bows and arrows. Others fought with lances. Others were specialists at tumbling rocks onto people down below. But these various specialties had to be meshed, because of course everybody showed up; mind you, they don't fight all year. And when they finally do show up they show up led by their own people with their own weapons.

If you are a professional military man who is thinking in campaign terms, and with the changes in any given campaign, this is obviously very inefficient. The spectacular thing is that at the coming of the Europeans, the bulk of the troops met the Europeans in this way. The groups were divided by ethnic groups with ethnic weapons under ethnic leadership. But clearly something else is needed, and

6. Felipe Guaman Poma de Ayala, *Nueva Corónica y Buen Gobierno* (Paris: Institut d'Ethnologie, 1936 [1613]).

7. Joan de Santa Cruz Pachacuti Yamqui Salcamaygua, "Relación de Antigüedades Deste Reyno del Perú," in *Crónicas Peruanas de Interés Indígena,* t. 209, ed. Francisco Esteve Barba (Madrid: Biblioteca de Autores Españoles, 1968 [1613]).

interestingly enough, before the coming of the Europeans—again we don't know at what point because neither the Chupaychu nor the Lupaqa have the beginning of any kind of a standing army. You do have the beginnings of a group of people permanently devoted to military services, just like the girls, plucked out of their normal, natural kinship and ethnic environment, transplanted and put somewhere else and dedicating their full life to military duties.

The way the Europeans interpret their functions, is of course the Praetorian guard, because if you have any kind of cross-cultural examples in 1532, you will hark inevitably back to Rome and Greece. But what is happening here we shouldn't be caught, trapped by the words. They were guards, sure they were guards. And the list I gave out [at the last lecture] is full of guards, guards; these are troops. Now, there is an interesting difference between the weaving women and the fighting men. The women are recruited everywhere, all over the place. Women who were attractive, women who were good-looking, women who were chief's daughters, women who in some way were selectable or selected. These [guards] come from one ethnic group only. And in this—I'm not too sure of, but so it seems. This is a[n] ethnic group which can be found till today, in the southern part of Ecuador, which was the last place the Incas were moving into just before the Europeans, and they had [put up] the most tremendous resistance with the coming of the Incas. Over and over again they had been defeated and defeated again and defeated again. One of our witnesses from the Lupaqa country who fought up here in Ecuador says the war lasted twenty years. He was there, and he brought back captives. We have some of these captives in the Lake Titicaca country.

But this group [the Cañari], not all of them, but a large number, in the thousands, [is] transplanted to Cuzco and put to full-time duties for the state, with their families. Where this was just a segregation of young women for a particular task, these men are brought over, and an important thing happens about all these changes that I am going to talk about today. Namely, as they are transplanted they are given land in the new places where they are settling. The institution is completely new, but the outfitting of the institution is done within the traditional framework. You do move them, but you treat them as if they were one more colonist group. The function is brand new; something really important is happening here. But the outward definition of this brand new group is still traditionally Andean. What they are made to do are new tasks, but they are given land, and there is no doubt whatever in their being here. It was quite independently of what the early boys say in 1542, [when] they are reported as one of the people miserable in the city because there is nothing for them to do. With the elite gone, with Tawantinsuyu destroyed, what does the king's guard do, what does the professional army do?

But there is one interesting thing about them which has not always been emphasized: that these people, from the beginning, side with the Europeans. The Europeans come in and these are the most reliable troops that the Europeans find as allies in the Andes. They shift their allegiance from the dynasty to the Europeans, and ever after, until they finally disappear, until they become Indians. Well, many of these people didn't know they were Indians. So, until they become Indians they are clearly distinguishable.

Now, what other people could be recruited? I'm interested in one feature of their past, I've mentioned it, is the fact that these are ex-rebels. These are people who resisted very hard. The recruitment of such resisters to the opposite force may have something to do with the eternal succession squabbles, which here, as in Africa, followed upon the death of the king. Since there is no rule of primogeniture or ultimogeniture, since the king has dozens of wives and hundreds of sons, and you can assume that only 10 percent of sons have reigning ambitions, you still have a very serious problem of who should succeed; and the moment when the Europeans arrive and find the succession squabble was in no way exceptional. Over and over again this has happened, and the Peruvian historian, Doña María Rostworowski, has suggested,[8] and I think quite sensibly, that the widely-touted incestuous marriages between brother and sister in the royal family had something to do with just this fact. If you limit succession only to the sons of the only queen, which is an incestuous queen, you're going to automatically eliminate 97 percent of all contenders, and the only people fighting it out are her sons—which inevitably reduces the number.

And now the setting up of this army has something to do with the succession squabbles, the setting up of the army has something to do with the fact that it happens in Ecuador. The whole study of the Tawantinsuyu trying to incorporate what today is Ecuador raises all kinds of interesting problems in economic expansion and in statecraft, which I have no time to go into, but just to attract your attention, that this was possible.

Now, as I said, for neither of the two groups [the aclla, the Cañari troops] is there any kind of precedent in the Lupaqa or the Chupaychu level of magnitude before. I'm not pretending that there were no models previously for these two groups. For all I know, somewhere there was. But it is interesting, at least, with the data so far, these seem to be innovations. And what's important here—the principle in common—is that for one group only, or for many groups, in both cases, you have people who no longer can work in their own community. And in the case of the women, they lose their motherly and wifely functions as they get transplanted and dragged out for state purposes. There is one possibility which [I] negate. No evidence, but we should think about it. Since these are innovations and they emphasize the power and the resources of the state, the possibility of this is one of those things the Incas may have learned from the hydraulic kingdoms of the north coast. That maybe, since crafts were apparently so well developed in the case of the north coast, that the Inca kings transplanted silversmiths from Chan Chan to Cuzco, the possibility of there being other craftsmen who were the model of this; the possibility that in the hydraulic kingdoms there were guards who had been plucked out of their ethnic background and put to full-time soldiering [is again a possibility]. I have no evidence for this, and I won't insist on it, but just remember it. And as we talk about what they could have learned from more rigid structures such as the irrigated kingdoms, this is the kind of thing that may have come from there.

All right, let me move on. I would like to put only one more group. I actually have a variety of groups; [on] some I have better evidence than on others, but I thought for our purposes today, three such groups would be adequate. There is one other group of, I think, great significance. As opposed to the previous two, the third group has earlier antecedents. You do find, as Morgan would say, the germs of thought behind the institutions; you can see them in earlier stages.

So, I come back then. You will remember that when I was talking [in the second lecture] about the different reciprocal services; the simplest one, the one in which no bookkeeping was kept of what I did for you and what you did for me, was known as *yanapay*. And the man performing the service becomes a *yanapaq* and the plural is *yanapaqkuna*. And then as the Europeans heard it they sort of condensed it, and it now becomes *yanacona*. There is a word used till today in [the] social structure of modern Peru, on the coast, particularly. Now these people, as I said, do have precedent. They exist both among the Chupaychu and among the Lupaqa. You will remember the Chupaychu situation; Chuchuyauri, a prominent man, lording over a few hundred households, maybe two hundred households, has not only four wives, but also four yanapaq, four yanapaqkuna. Of these four, one is above, one is below, and two are right there with him in the village. The important thing about him, you'll remember I said [in the third lecture], is that those two men are the only other men besides Chuchuyauri himself to be polygynous. The functions

---

8. Rostworowski, María. "Sucesiones, Correinado e incesto real entre los Incas." In María Rostworowski, *Ensayos de historia andina I*, (Lima: Instituto de Estudios Peruanos, 2005).

they perform are numerous and they are obviously men of responsibility. They are reliable men, and one important thing in European times, they are protected by the fact that they are at this time in court. We can't really talk about the court; a court made up of four wives and four retainers [yanapaqkuna], two of whom are away anyway, isn't much of a court. But again, if we're thinking in Morganian terms, if we're looking for germs of what is to come in the future, here it is, in its smallest and its most embryonic form. I then thought I would distribute among you what happens to these people on a much larger scale. Once you have a whole kingdom, then of course the situation becomes different.

In Table 2,[9] [the single horizontal line that runs across the width of the table separates information about the Upper Qari dynasty kings from the Lower Kusi dynasty kings]. In [the] columns called Acora and Juli, you will see that the[se] towns say that, in addition to everybody working a few days all year—in addition to the men of service, sixty [in Chucuito, for the Qari dynasty] and, [down here in the second set of headings] forty-seven [in Chucuito, for the Kusi dynasty]—you then have [in the Acora Qari column]: "To his grandfather they gave ten Indians, for *anaconas*." And the other town [the Juli Qari column]: "To his grandfather they gave ten Indians once and for all, and he uses their descendants." These men, at the time of the European inspection [number] sixty ["Indians of service"] in Chucuito].[10] And one very important thing—which in a manuscript I wrote some years ago, I spent page after page after page wondering as to—were these people married or not? Because part of their conditional dependency and servitude was: were they married, did they have households? And I had to spend all those pages because I had no data. Fortunately since then we have some data and those pages are useless. What is happening here—obviously these people are married, all maintain households and, importantly, they belong to the normal ethnic groups residing in those areas. These are not captives. In addition to these there are some captives, but I have no information on the social condition of the captives. I don't know what the captives did. I don't know what the fates of the children of the captives were. So I have kept them out of these Tables 2 and 3.

Table 3, which takes just one subdivision, one-seventh, of the whole Lupaqa kingdom, shows you that this centenary informant Vilpa Cutipa, says that his father had twenty retainers, of both moieties who were Uru, and fifteen are still alive, and he also had ten Aymara, and the others have died—so he probably had more. So clearly, the court here is larger. As the political unit grows and has control of more ecological islands all over the country, so it has more people doing full time and hereditary work for the kingdom in this particular situation. Now, one thing we can do with this data, which does not affect, by the way, at all, the Incaic situation but is interesting in itself—what this data shows you is the proportion of people. For the first time we have some actual quantitative measurement of how many such dependents there were. In the case of the Lupaqa, they form about one percent of the population.

Now this is very small, and yet it is important, because the debate about slavery and the debate about how slavery could be an explanation of the economy of the Andes is of course one which has already

---

9.   Murra refers to a table he published in "An Aymara Kingdom in 1567" (1968a); it is reproduced here in Fig. 14.

10.   The text between square brackets [ ] corresponds to the sole Murra/LHM Lecture text in this volume that HL and FYW edited for publication. During the lecture, Murra read from a published Table 2 (reproduced here as Fig. 14), paper copies of which he had distributed to the audience. In our opinion the text, as transcribed, is unclear and Murra, in discussing the tabulated data, seems unfamiliar with standard vocabulary used in describing the organization of a table of this kind. JVM's original text, as captured and transcribed from the reel-to reel tape of Lecture 4, appears here:

> Look at the Table 2. Table 2, at the bottom of the first horizontal thing, in columns called Acora and Juli you will see that the towns say that in addition to everybody working a few days all year, in addition to the men of service sixty and forty-seven, you then have: To his grandfather they gave ten Indians, for *anaconas*. And the other town, to his grandfather they gave ten Indians once and for all, and he uses their descendants. These men, at the time of the European inspection, are sixty.

begun and will grow more important in years to come. On the whole, it seems to me that one percent of the economy, assuming the yanapaqkuna are slaves—and I don't think the evidence on that is very strong—but even if you assume they are, this is a very low proportion, and we are very far from being able to classify this economy as a slave economy, comma; nevertheless, we should remember that quantity is not always the most important thing. If we're thinking in terms of major changes to come, the fact that the group is very small now does not mean that it could not grow in years to come and, more specifically, if the percentage was not higher when we're dealing with Tawantinsuyu. I cannot answer if the percentage was higher at the state level than at the Cuzco level or not, but I think we should at least be aware of the fact that it could be higher at the state level and under certain conditions could grow quite rapidly, particularly if the pressures for revenue would be important.

This raises the kind of point: Were these yanapaqkuna active in a critical sector of Lupaqa or Andean economy, or were they just another example of luxury? Were they just, like the four women, part of a symbolic statement about how important this man is, and on the other hand, the four women are very hardworking because they're making beer all the time. So between the status and their very practical contribution they made, you could think of these four [yanapaqkuna] obviously as this same level. It's a way of getting certain kinds of work which you can't marry; herding work—for example—and incorporating them into this unit. At that point, if the yanapaqkuna of the state were of the same kind, then they are not in a critical sector of the economy and it doesn't matter. But note in Table 2 (Fig. 14)—that the people working for the king for the year [are] young men before marriage—in the very first column where you see [a total of] sixty: ten of them are herders; twenty-five are trying to control or are working in the oasis on the coast, raising maize; fifteen help him with his agricultural chores; and only ten are at his house. Now you see, this is really an important difference. You have a majority engaged in the very critical aspects of the economy, and in the lower moiety kingdom, there are seventeen herders of the [total of] forty-seven. Now, if herding is of the importance that I think it might possibly have in the south—not elsewhere, but in the south—these enormous herds of fifty thousand, [of] a hundred thousand head, you might very well think here, of major shifts, of major changes in the total picture of how Andean economics should be distributed, governed. And in that case, if your herders are the yanapaqkuna, if the yanapaqkuna in fact have emerged out of a herding situation, then they could be very important for the future, even if at the moment when we catch them, they're still a very small minority. I cannot answer it for the state; I can only tell you what is true for the Lupaqa.

The condition of hereditary servitude is an important one. One of the earliest European observers, who was a very, very perspicacious observer, Pedro Cieza de León,[11] refers to them always as "criados perpetuos"[12] and this has generally been the roots of why some people feel that we are dealing here with a real slave situation. The Lupaqa data are, although very limited, are nevertheless very tantalizing, because the Lupaqa man essentially argues that these people fit this pattern. What he says is: observe the root of this whole word. He is not the slave. He is not described as a person who doesn't have access to the strategic goods of his society. He is not described as a man without rights. He is clearly married and with children. He is living in the community and he is incorporated at least into the moiety [system]; it's unclear if they're in the lineage system as well, but they're clearly in the moiety [system]. But it all

11. Pedro de Cieza de León, *El Señorío de los Incas. Segunda Parte de la Crónica del Perú.* (Lima: Instituto de Estudios Peruanos, 1967 [1553]).

12. In *The Economic Organization of the Inka State*, Murra notes "Cieza defines the *yana* as "perpetual servants" ["criados perpetuos"] (1980a: 165).

Revenues of the two Lupaqa kings, compiled from data in the
Visita Hecha a La Provincia de Chucuito por Garci Diez de San Miguel en el Año 1567

		CHUCUITO	ACORA	ILAVE	JULI	POMATA	YUNGUYO	ZEPITA
The QARI kings of the Upper or Alasaa moiety had access to:	LAND	70-100 *tupu* of land "planted by all of them" (f. 9r p.20)	20 *tupu*	20 *tupu*	20 *tupu*	20 *tupu*	20 *tupu*	20 *tupu*
	CLOTH	"when asked they weave for them five pieces of cloth" (f. 9r p.20)	"1-2 *kumbi* cloths 6-7 *awaska*" (f. 9r p.20)	the same	the same	the same	the same	the same
	INDIANS OF SERVICE (*mit'ani*)	"60 Indians of service: 10 herders 25 in Moquegua [on coast] 15 in his fields 10 in his house plus 2 to carry wood, grass" (f. 9v p.21)	"3 Indians of service" (f. 10r p.22)	"3 Indians of service" (f. 10r p.22)	?	?	?	?
	YANA (*anaconas*)		"to his grandfather they gave 10 Indians for *anaconas*" (f. 45v p.93)		"to his grandfather they gave 10 Indians... once and for all... and he uses their decendants" (f. 58r p.117-118)			
The KUSI kings of the Lower or Maasaa moiety had access to:	LAND	50 *tupu*	5 *tupu*	2 *tupu*	6 *tupu*	10 *tupu*	7 *tupu*	7 *tupu*
	CLOTH	12 pieces of cloth	1 of *kumbi* 2 of *awaska*	4 pieces	6 pieces	3-4 pieces	3-4 pieces	3 pieces
	INDIANS OF SERVICE (*mit'ani*)	"47 Indians of service: 17 herders 15 at Moquegua, Sama 11 in his fields 2 in his house plus 2 for wood"	7 of service	3 of service	11 Indians	10 Indians	11 Indians	11 Indians
	YANA (*anaconas*)		"to his ancestors... they gave him certain Indians for *anaconas*..." (f. 48v p.99-100)					

(table after Murra 1968)

Figure 14. Chart of the revenues of the two Lupaqa kings, as reported in the *Visita* of Garci Diez de San Miguel in 1567 (Murra 1968a: Table II, 129).

comes from helping without book-keeping; it comes from the most familiar, the most intimate kind of reciprocity.

Now, much as has been said here, this is part of a public relations job that they [the state] are doing, they are defining these poor girls who will never see home again as being selected, and they're defining these men who are doing all these ugly tasks that must be done as their most familiar and intimate kind of helpers. But for one very interesting thing in the Lupaqa material: he says that the sons of the yana-paqkuna are not all fit to be taken to be yanapaq. If the first son, he says, is unfit, he is sent back to the village. And the second one is moved in, assuming he is fit. The notion of fitness, the notion that there are certain kinds of qualities or characteristics or skills or who knows what. We don't know any more than that—this is the desperation of this kind of [ethnohistoric] work, is that this is just the very beginning of it, this is the only source that deals functionally with this kind of social categories. The possibility that they are hereditary—but not the whole group, not the whole household, not all the siblings; that every-thing goes by ones, which fits the Andean pattern very well, that you only send one person. Everybody goes in turn. Everything is done by mit'a. And mit'a means something done cyclically and in turn.

Now you see, if not all sons inherit this particular dependent and deprived status, this changes the whole picture. We are confronted with something very different than what we thought maybe, at first. This may work here; it may not work at the Inca level, we don't know, but there is enough here again for us to think very hard about it. Finally, and crucially, these people unmistakably at the Lupaqa level have access to the good things of life. They have land, they have herds, they have boats—dugouts—they have all kinds of things which are considered desirable that everybody else has. They may very well have less. They may be deprived in some ways as yet undefined. All kinds of limitations on their lives are expectable since these are clearly, even by Andean standards, low-status groups. But there is no reason to immedi-ately assume that what you're confronted here is with a slave community, and the important thing is to really go out and try to understand what is happening.

I hope your resistance is good because I have quite a bit of material still to cover. I don't know if you are as interested in all these groups as I am. I think they're fascinating because they changed the whole definition [of *yana*] so much.

Let me move quickly to the yanapaqkuna of the state. I know much less about them so all I will do is give you a few hints of what kind of things we do know. The oral tradition of the dynasty which the Europeans record is categorical—that the Incas invented this condition. Now obviously this is nonsense; this must have gone on for generations before the Incas. But the oral tradition says a queen invented it. Generally speaking, the Incas attribute everything onerous, everything difficult, everything that nobody would like in his right mind to do, to the queen's intervention. It is she who thinks up all these terrible ways of treating people. What happened is that the brother of the king, sent out to conduct the census, cheats. He does not report a whole bunch of people, and those people he hides for a succession war that he was planning. Of course he is discovered, a drum is made out of him, and they begin to punish all the people who have been guilty, you see. They are defined now as rebels. And they begin to be killed and their houses destroyed.

At some point the queen says, "Don't you think it would be more sensible to put all these people to work instead of having to end up killing them?" According to oral tradition it dawns upon the right folks that this was a great idea, and that's what they do. And ever after we've had the yanapaqkuna. Now all of this legend is of no importance to me but for two things. One, the attribution of all these things in one more case to the queen, which I think will turn out [to be] the importance of it. And the second thing is the definition of these people as rebels. Because this is one thing we know, that through all this system, as much as oral tradition can reach back through it, there is continuous rebellion. And if anything, oral tradition has an interest in minimizing rebellion. Oral tradition that is particularly recited to the Europeans has an interest of dampening, of ignoring, of sidestepping rebellion, yet there is tremendous and continuous rebellion all through the kingdom and this is how you deal with rebels. The possibility [is] that many of the yanapaqkuna at the state level are people who are either actual rebels or potential rebels or "rebels" simply in quotation marks, but these poor fellows simply were not enumerated, not of their own free will, apparently. When convenient, you can reduce somebody to yanapaq status by declaring him a rebel. And that seems to me to be interesting and deserves attention.

Now, this does not mean that among the yanapaqkuna you didn't have people of high status. Or of high governmental responsibilities, much as these two men at the village level are clearly responsible and serious people who are trusted with many, many activities. What is true of all of them, all those we can get any hint of, is that they are relieved of reciprocal services within their own communities. As the Europeans say, they are removed from the tribute rolls. They, like the women, like the soldiers, stopped being members of their ethnic communities. They no longer owed reciprocal services to the traditional authorities and are transferred on a full-time basis to a state chore. I think every other option is open. The function that is important here—not the details, we'll figure out the details in fifty years to come—what is important here is the searching which takes out all these categories and many others that I haven't burdened you with, that takes them out from their traditional ethnic unit, that removes them from reciprocal services, their own authorities can no longer count on them, their own brothers can no longer count on them, in the case of the women they will never be anybody's wife or mother in the village—and it is this removal, this not being enumerated in the census anymore—that is really important and that creates new people, new energies that can work resources on a full-time basis for the state; and it is this which is new.

All these categories and what they can do, the functions they can perform, their productivity, their new productivities, this is now virtually full-time productivity. Not quite, but virtually full-time productivity, this is what is important. The break with the kinship reckoning is what's important, and not at this point the details of how they did it.

One passing characteristic, I have a long list but I will skip it. At the moment in the succession squabble, when one of the brothers is ahead and he gets his hands on the wives of his competitor, all the wives are killed, all the children are killed, and they don't stop with the king unit, they begin killing the yanapaqkuna of the king and they kill up to a point at which point they say: well from here on in the rest don't matter so much, they don't count so much. The affiliation of the group, at least of the yanapaqkuna, to the person of the given king brings us back to the list that I distributed in the third lecture, where you noted that certain people are responsible for the mummy of one of the kings, or certain of the other group there of ten people, ... [are responsible for] the weapons of one of the dead kings. These very private retainer kinds of services which are part ceremonial, part economic, part political, all these things are all mixed up in there somewhere, and the killing of the yanapaqkuna of an important figure in a political field seems to show you, at the political level, [something] similar to what you have here. These are presumably retainers who have lost all of their rights as ordinary villagers, but they have gained, since they now can be polygynous, since they now have pan-village or pan-ethnic group responsibilities. It is very possible that the functional definition of these yanapaqkuna, even at the state level, had something to do with the person of the ruler and of performing services of a more personal kind. The very possibility that you have at the court of Louis XIV the duke holding the pants which the ruler will wear today—that kind of a personal retainership is very possibly involved here and that line of division, who do you kill when you kill the kinfolk of the dead king and who escapes, is something again to watch and to follow through.

Now, to go back to the larger problem of Tawantinsuyu. As it expands, as the state's needs grow, you obviously have to have new sources of energy. Inevitably in this kind of society, new sources of energy mean new social categories that will respond to the new people doing new kinds of tasks. I have no idea of how old this particular institution [the yanapaqkuna] is. We have them at the local level, we have them at the larger level, we have them at the state level. I do not think that it is terribly important for us at this point to define when they started and what was the first activity that made it possible—maybe herding made it possible in one case—but I would not insist that everywhere throughout the state [there is] the possibility that this was another thing that came from the coastal irrigation kingdoms. But I would say the kind of sermon that Moses Finley[13] teaches us, about not worrying so much about slave and free, but being concerned about all the different interstitial positions, everything that remains between state and free, all the various kind of functional arrangements, and all the differing kinds of statuses that can exist with what is, at least overtly, defined as a dependent status. This is, I think, where we should look.

That, of course, and the other question I asked earlier, how critical a sector of the economy is involved. If there are people holding the king's pants, they are unimportant in the larger picture. If there are people engaged in herding, in irrigation, in agriculture, then this is a very different thing, and you can easily contemplate the possibility of this group expanding, the possibility of true slaves emerging and then really very fundamental changes are possible. I have said already that all these people had in common one important thing. They have been withdrawn from the lineages. They have been withdrawn from the villages, from their ethnic groups. They no longer owe any services to the king like they used to, but they also owe nothing anymore to their brothers, they owe nothing anymore to their local Chuchuyauris, and this is a real loss.

It is a loss, I suggest to you, very similar to the loss that the community and the ethnic group suffered at the time of the Inca conquest. You remember that in addition to new resources created by the kingdom through irrigation, through terracing, through the irrigation of rivers and other activities, I said that they set up at that time islands of resources throughout the kingdom that were alienated from local groups. It is here that you have a comparison. Just like islands of resources were alienated, so now you have people being alienated, human energies taken out, creatures taken completely out, plucked out and assigned to these new tasks; and the alienation of the peoples, of course, is a serious drain on the energies of the groups they have left behind. It is most dramatic in the case of the women, but certainly important in the case, I think, of all of them.

You have in that sense a tribute here. You remember the question asked of me after the third lecture, why didn't they go to a tribute system, and I answered—but I did not answer, of course, because I don't really know why they did not go on to a tribute system. But I suggest to you one thing they are doing here, there is a tribute, a permanent tribute, not just a temporary one, a permanent tribute in people, who are removed and forever after lost to their communities, at least at a state level. Even assuming that the Lupaqa would feed some of their young back to the community at the state level, apparently all of the children inherited their parents' status. The ability to withdraw people, the ability to take people out is

---

13.   Moses Finley, *The World of Odysseus* (New York: Viking Press, 1954); See also: Moses Finley, *The Ancient Economy* (Berkeley: University of California Press, 1973); Peter Garnsey, Keith Hopkins, and C.R. Whittaker, editors, *Trade in the Ancient Economy* (London: Chatto and Windus, 1983).

comparable then, it seems to me, to the setting up of state resources and comparable also to the fiction by which all land everywhere is now the property of the crown, is now the property of the state. You are now making all people—specifically, only the yanapaqkuna—but in the long run you have established a principle that you can withdraw these three and many more, and in the long run this can very easily affect everybody else. Just like the legal fiction that all lands are the king's may not be enforced on any given day, but it is there in reserve, it can be plotted out when needed and can be used when convenient. For one thing, you punish the rebel and you punish a rebel, not only by killing them all but by taking up their lands, and these lands once available to you are available for many purposes, not just for productive purposes.

Now what is really happening here is that you are incorporating land and energies, land and people into an economic sphere in which they were not present previously in the Andes. In the past, certain things could be traded back and forth, exchanged, bartered, provided in certain ways, but land and people remained always in the hands of the ethnic group. It was one sphere which was a sphere of kinship relations, a sphere of ethnic loyalties, it was a sphere of reciprocal services. There are now some people, some lands, yet maybe someday all people, all lands, are removed from that sphere of reciprocal services and kinship and put into another sphere which is constantly growing, the sphere of the state. We are confronted there with the major break. We are confronted here with the moment when we are watching this break. It was just the kind of situation that, if Lewis Henry Morgan could have had a chance to observe and to study, I think it would not be farfetched to assume that he would have been delighted to have a chance to observe this particular situation.

The alienation of lands and the alienation of people makes possible a new kind of redistribution. You see, the fact that they now have done something, quotes, "unprecedented," something unheard of, namely taking people out forever, not just temporarily, not just on a rotation system, not just on reciprocal services, but this permanent plucking out and putting them into a new category does not mean the distribution stops because after you have moved the people, after you have moved the resources to this new category, redistribution continues. You handle these new things as if they were a traditional item of redistribution, as if they are cloth, as if they are food, as if they are beer, and once you have them in this category, you can do things that you could never do as long as they were in category A. You can now give it away, you can give them away, you can give away people, and this is one of the most fundamental changes which is happening, and I don't think there is much precedent before.

This is quite a new situation. Under the old system food, cloth, beer, hospitality, could all be offered to the deserving, people who had in some way been merited from the state could get all these things. Towards the end what is included in this category of free redistribution are unmistakably people and the people come from these categories. The most desirable folks that you could possibly give away are the weaving women, partly of course because not all of them wove, I am exaggerating, I call them the weaving women because it suits my whim, but clearly they did other things, and remember that they were of many different statuses. I do not care if there were four or six [statuses], it does not matter for our purposes. The fact is that some of them were of high status and had been selected not from some village, but have been selected from the very royal lineages. The award of a woman from a royal lineage to one of the defeated dukes or kings as the kingdom spreads becomes one more method of creating alliances. Much as in the older days, from the very beginning the king at the center is constantly marrying women from every one of the defeated groups. Those of you who know African ethnology know how many parallels there are to this situation. But it isn't just that you incorporate women from all these communities, it is also that you are giving away women, and the women you give away are the women defined legally in this category who can be given away since they have now been plucked out of their normal kinship and ethnic situations and become a state resource.[14]

It seems to me that Andean civilization, as seen at this moment when the European invasion occurs, this traumatic moment, would have had many other reasons to interest Lewis Henry Morgan. Now Leslie White, in one of the most interesting things he did, which was the introduction to the correspondence between [Adolph F.] Bandelier and Lewis Henry Morgan[15]—I don't know, I imagine you in Rochester read Morgan all the time, but at least you could—that is among the many things that have been done in the Morgan corpus, and one of the most interesting things to me, because what it shows, if you remember, those of you who remember, is that gradually Morgan convinced young Bandelier— who had been raised in his [Morgan's] own household—that his perception of Mexican statecraft was inaccurate. That what we had is not what the Europeans said, "king," and that there weren't those big fancy markets, and there weren't all those armies, and there weren't all those features of complexity, but this was just another chiefdom, this was just another unit like the southwestern Pueblos, or maybe the Cheyenne, or at best the Iroquois Confederacy. Now this is one way in which Morgan misunderstood American statecraft and the American kingdoms, and his critique is, of course, a justified critique. I will not elaborate on it, it has been done very well by others.

A more recent critique of Morgan in this whole area has been one published by a French colleague, Maurice Godelier. Maurice Godelier[16] has been interested in what was the Asiatic mode of production of Marx and Engels before Engels published his *Origin of the Family*,[17] and he notices that Marx gets the idea early in the fifties. It appears in the correspondence between Marx and Engels, it appears in the early Marx books. All the way [to] and including *Capital* he endorses this whole idea that there is a separate avenue towards civilization which is not the one we are familiar with—of tribal followed by slavery, followed by feudalism, by capitalism and by socialism, that there must be other avenues. For forty years Marx and Engels both in their various letters and publications are aware that there may very well be a completely different avenue towards civilization, and that this Asiatic mode of production is characterized by a few interesting things, interesting for our situation here, namely, that the local village and ethnic communities remain quite self-sufficient and considerably independent, and yet are fitted into a larger, superordinate organization which can be a Maharajah, which can be a king, which can be a temple, which can be a Han of some sort who extracts certain kinds of tribute and may occasionally even conduct some productive operation and irrigation canal. But on the whole you don't have slavery in any important economic way—if there are a few slaves, they are of this kind, they are attached to the actual houses of the mighty—slavery is an unimportant phenomenon. There are no feudal type relationships between local individual dukes and [their] vassals, so they were aware that this was neither slavery nor

---

14. In her discussion of the *aclla*, Irene Silverblatt underscores Murra's argument about the Inca state's redistribution of people and the giving away of women (1987).

15. Leslie A. White, ed., *Pioneers in American Anthropology: the Bandelier-Morgan Letters, 1873-1883*. (Albuquerque: University of New Mexico Press, 1940).

16. Maurice Godelier, *La Notion de "Mode de Production Asiatique" et les Schémas d'Évolution des Sociétés* (Paris: Centre d'Études et de Recherches Marxistes, 1975 [1964]). See also: *Las Sociedades Primitivas y el Nacimiento de las Sociedades de Clases Según Marx y Engels: Un Balance Crítico*, trans. Mario Arrubla y Jorge Orlando Melo (Bogotá: La Oveja Negra, 1987 [1969]).

17. Friedrich Engels, *The Origin of the Family, Private Property and the State: In the Light of the Researches of Lewis H. Morgan*, trans. Ernest Untermann (Chicago: Charles H. Kerr, 1902 [1884]). Engels began work on this book after having read Karl Marx's handwritten notes on Lewis Henry Morgan's 1877 volume, *Ancient Society: or, Researches in the Lines of Human Progress from Savagery, Through Barbarism to Civilization* (1877).

was it feudalism. It didn't at all fit the pattern of development of the Europeans' scheme that they were familiar with, and for twenty years they keep talking, never in any major way, never more than a page or two, but consistently, about this separate avenue.

According to Godelier, what really happened was that once they discovered ancient society, they become convinced. The argument, interestingly enough, according to Godelier, is that what convinced them was not so much the demonstration about the Aztecs and the Incas, since they had no data on either the Aztecs or the Incas—you would be surprised as to how many references there are to the Incas in Marx's *Capital*, you put them all together and you have at least fifteen paragraphs—but they weren't interested in that. What they liked about Morgan's argument was that Morgan provided them with an explanation they found very exciting about the classical work, and particularly about the early Greek city-states and the early Greek principalities, and since that was material they controlled, because they could read Greek and Latin and having had a classical education were familiar with this argument, Morgan was so convincing about reducing some of the so-called Greek kingdoms to the kind of Iroquois things they apparently were. I have not checked this material and so I do not know.

They were perfectly willing then to accept Morgan's argument that whatever was true for these early Greek princes, dukes and chieftains was equally true for the Aztecs and the Inca, and this is how, when the *Origin of the Family* finally comes out in 1884, there is no trace whatever of the Asiatic mode of production until much later when in Germany and with Wittfogel[18] the discussion reopens. I have no time to go into that, I have been reading on it for preparation of this because I discovered it only as I was thinking of these lectures.

So you see, you have all these criticisms of Morgan, either because he influenced Marx and in turn, until today, the Soviet Union's hard time with this whole notion that there might be a separate ethnic padding for evolution beyond the classical one. The arguments of Leslie White about how wrong Morgan was in pressuring Bandelier and changing Bandelier's mind are, of course, all quite true. But I would like to suggest to you that the only thing Morgan had available about the kind of societies that interests us in this series, the Mesoamerican and the Andean societies, was very limited. He had only one tactic available to him, namely the perusal of European reports, and what was available in the sixties and seventies is what was available to Prescott.[19] Now I think Prescott made better use of that material than Morgan did, but still it was very, very few [sources]. We have a great deal more, but most importantly, we now have a multitactical approach to any kind of these early American civilizations. We are no longer at the mercy of the reports of the European scribes, missionaries and soldiers. Even when we have European data, we have brand new kinds of European data, the bureaucratic documents, the land litigation documents, the kind of sources which are in common use in economic history all over the world. They are now available. But much more importantly we now know that archaeology can provide a degree of refinement, a degree of information, both quantitative and qualitative, which was unthinkable even when I was a graduate student. We now know from the linguistic material. We now know about—at least in the Andes, if not everywhere—in the Andes the very strong reality of ethnologic continuities, of ethnology today, just like linguistics today can provide you with a vast amount of information relevant to the kind of problems that Morgan and Marx and Engels were facing in mid-nineteenth century.

As we use every tactic we come to a situation which I am sure Lewis Henry Morgan would have appreciated, and we might have even convinced him to look again at this material and reconsider his appreciation.

---

18.   Karl A. Wittfogel, *Oriental Despotism: A Comparative Study of Total Power* (New Haven: Yale University Press, 1957).

19.   William H. Prescott, *History of the Conquest of Peru* (Philadelphia: Lippincott, 1847).

We are confronted in Andean civilization with a whole series of civilizations. Inevitably in this kind of a short presentation, it is the series, the multiplicity of societies is slighted, is inevitably worn down; but one should remember that we are confronted with a series of civilizations, which are active and creative along both avenues that Morgan talked about, on which he recommended investigation. You will remember that Morgan saw development and growth proceeding along two quite different lines and each deserving an investigation in its own right. On the one hand inventions, on the one hand technological progress, the discovery of new ways of utilizing resources and of new ways of perceiving resources which have never been seen before. In the case of the Andes you are confronted here with a brand new completely pristine form of agriculture.

There is nothing here shared with any other part of the world. Whatever was created here was Andean-ly domesticated, Andean-ly mastered and grown by Andean people for Andean purposes. Not only that the mastery of this incredible series of environments—most of them inhospitable and requiring a great deal of energy and a great deal of ingenuity to master—this also was present and was proceeding very fast. As archaeology goes further, you see that communities arise at higher and higher and higher levels, which means that you are producing potatoes and other tubers at higher and higher and higher [altitudes], and therefore more difficult circumstances.

I won't go on with this avenue of inventions because we have done so little with it. We have worked so hard, let's say on the pottery which we need for chronological periodization, but there is so much more, and so much more fundamental stuff to be learned about how society and civilization grew in the Andes along the line of invention.

But remember that there is another avenue that Morgan advocated, the avenue of institutional development, the kind of institutions that arise. And here I must remind you that whatever arose here, whatever states, cities, armies, kings and the technology that arose, the productivity that was created here was all done on [...] what I consider an Afro-American model, a model which is absent in Asia and in Europe. [In the Andes], where you get civilization without any animals, because I do not consider the llama of any significant difference. [There are] no animals anywhere in the New World or in Africa that provide the energy necessary to pull and push and haul, and no technological things which are symbolized for the Europeans by the wheel.

This is the "no beasts, no wheel" model of achieving civilization, and inevitably as these extra non-human, parahuman energies are absent, the way you are going to get civilization is by beating it out of people. Somehow you will have to convince people that they have to work harder, that they will have to work longer, that they will have to work in new and different ways. It is not along machine-like areas that the Andean environment was subjected; the technology was a very simple technology. What was different here was how people were organized,[20] how people were manipulated, how people were cajoled and convinced, and pushed and forced to produce all these things that had to be done, and how these institutions developed. How they got people—because they couldn't do it just through the whip. The position that somehow all this can be explained through a position of slavery and everybody was a slave and doing this just under a whip seems to me to be much, much too simple. Of course, what the real system of social economic organization was you have seen. I can give you only hints, I cannot really explain it. But it is important to see in the absence of beasts, and in the absence of machinery, the way you are reaching civilization is through the manipulation of social and economic categories and the manipulation of people which are, if not completely unique here, certainly have been pushed here with these resources and these circumstances further I think than anywhere else.

---

20. Lechtman argues that organization, itself, is a primary component of technology (cf. Lechtman 1993).

Finally, when the Europeans come in 1532, when the European invasion, the European blight hits this particular area, what we are confronted with—and we can evaluate what is happening here—we are at the very crucial moment, we are at the moment when the old reciprocal and distributive bonds bringing these people together are stretched way beyond anything comparable elsewhere. The organizational relationships are still discernable, you can still easily see the reciprocal obligation, you can see very well when the king gives away lands; for example, it is a man who is in some way meriting this land because of the service to the king that gets it. But one of the Europeans, one of the very smart Europeans says: but notice that when the original beneficiary dies, the land reverts to the lineage, not the lineage that originally was there, but to the lineage of the dead beneficiary. So it gets fitted right back into the traditional system, new things emerge, but the new things emerge, as you well know, from other situations of change [and] do not necessarily mean that all the old is replaced; the new comes and affects the old and the old is changed by the new and in turn affects and encompasses the new as it emerges. And while the first is distorted, namely this reciprocal redistributive marginal exchange kind of society, simultaneously you have completely new institutions: the possible emergence of a large percentage of yanapaqkuna, the importance of the colonies which I haven't burdened you with today, but the colonists are very important. If the state colonists were five percent of the population of course it doesn't matter so much, but suppose, like some people say, thirty, forty, fifty percent of the population in some areas were. John Rowe[21] thinks that. Waldemar Espinoza[22] thinks that in some areas more than fifty percent of the people were no longer the original inhabitants, but were new people moved there for state purposes.

Assuming that the change had gone as profoundly as that, you clearly have the emergence here of brand new institutions, of brand new statuses, of brand new productivities, and all of this, I think, would have enchanted Morgan and might very well have encouraged him to reconsider the larger picture he had, so wrong but still so creative, about Mesoamerican and Andean civilizations.

Thank you.

---

21.   Ibid. Footnote 2.
22.   Waldemar Espinoza Soriano, possibly a personal communication with Murra.

Glossary

In the text and in this glossary, Quechua and Aymara words are spelled as Murra wrote them in his publications from the 1960s onward. These spellings are influenced both by his earlier study of colonial authors, who rendered Inka lexicon in Spanish orthography, and by the modern linguistic study of Quechua which was then taking shape at Cornell and elsewhere. (Murra's Quechuist colleague at Cornell was Donald Solá.) The forms in square brackets are later reconstructions of Inka forms using the orthographic system promulgated in 1971 by Peru's President Juan Velasco Alvarado.

[A. Aymara, Q. Quechua, S. Spanish]

aclla [Q. *aqlla, aqllakuna* plural]   Young women chosen by the Inka as full-time retainers of the state. Removed from their communities, they were housed in Cuzco or in state administrative centers. Their principal responsibility was spinning and weaving the finest *qumpi* cloth for the king's personal clothing, which the king often distributed as special state gifts.

awasqa [Q.]   Plain woven cloth. The corvée duty that a community woman head of household owed to the Inka annually was one garment she wove of plain cloth, used primarily for the army.

ayllu [Q.]   An enduring, named, localized group of households sharing genealogical and/or ritual identity on lines of inheritance. *Ayllus* function as segments of a larger community or polity. A household's *ayllu* membership implies land/water use rights and labor exchange duties, both within the localized kin grouping, and with other *ayllu* of the same community.

ayni [Q.]	A service that is performed with the expectation of symmetrical, measured reciprocity. An *ayni* network consists of long-standing peer or neighbor relationships involving mutual exchange. The term *ayni* implies equitable repayment in kind, whether positive compensation for help, or "payback" for harm.
cacique [S.]	Spanish word for *kuraka*.
camayoc [Q. *kamayuq*]	Official or manager (as in *khipu kamayuq*), or knot makers, managers of *khipu* records; also, highly knowledgeable and notable specialist craftspeople (as in *qumpi kamayuq*), or weaver of fine q*umpi* cloth.
ch'arqui [Q. *ch'arki*]	Freeze-dried meat, often llama meat.
ch'uñu [Q.]	Freeze-dried luki potatoes (bitter potatoes).
cumbi [Q. *qumpi*]	Woven cloth of the finest quality made by *qumpi kamayuq*s, full-time women and men retainers of the Inka state. *Aqlla* (women) wove *qumpi* cloth for the personal clothing of the Inka king and royals. *Qumpi kamayuk*s also wove other types of cloth for the state's political use, as diplomatic gifts.
curaca [Q. *kuraka*]	Headman or leader of a community; local lord; head of an *ayllu*.
encomendero [S.]	A colonial Spaniard granted an *encomienda* trusteeship over a group of Andean people. *Encomienda* included responsibility for their welfare and religious conversion in exchange for the right to collect tribute from them, in labor and in kind.
mallku [A.]	Aymara word, equivalent to *kuraka*.
mañanakuy [Q.]	A ceremony that accompanies the reentry of a *suyu* of land after lying fallow. "Ritual offerings to the lords of the mountains are often accompanied with a mañay request for a counter-prestation of fertile lands" (Manneheim 1991: 91).
mañay [Q.]	A prestation that receives a counter-prestation in kind; "that which one must lend, that which must be asked for" (Murra 1980: 192).

manta [S.]	Blanket, large shawl
mit'a [Q.]	Labor "loaned" to a collectivity for a term, as when one contributes 'a turn' to a community or state levy. Reciprocal compensation may be asymmetrical or even purely symbolic, depending on status inequalities. But the beneficiary in any case must reciprocate with food (feasting) and chicha (maize beer).
mit'ani [A.]; *mitayo* [Q. *mit'ayuq*]	A person who performs mit'a labor. Both terms were used by Spaniards to designate Andean peoples working for them under conditions of forced labor, notably in gold, mercury, and silver mining.
mitima [Q. *mitmaq, mitmaqkuna*, plural]	Resettled colonists. The Inka resettled large numbers of Andean peoples throughout the empire as colonists committed to agro-pastoral and craft production and to staffing frontier forts and internal garrisons.
mullu [Q.]	Marine shell, used primarily in reference to *Spondylus princeps* (the "thorny oyster") and Strombus (the shell trumpet). Both mollusks, native to the warm waters off the coast of Ecuador, were brought from Ecuador by the Inka in large quantities as an exchange item. *Spondylus*-shell *mullu* was a sacred, living material that brought rain when offered to the gods.
panaca [Q. *panaka*]	A royal Inka *ayllu* or kin group. At the time of the Spanish invasion, the Inka reckoned 10 *panaka*s, each descended from a deceased Inka king (mythical or historical).
qollqa [Q. *qullqa*]	Storehouse
quipu [Q. *khipu*]	Knotted string accounting device employed in record-keeping throughout the Inka empire (e.g., for census-taking, for records of corvée-owing households).
suyu [Q.]	In sectorial fallowing or *raymi*, a sector of agricultural land that reenters the cultivation cycle after having lain fallow; also, region, delimited area.

Tahuantinsuyu [Q. *Tawantinsuyu*]   The Inka name for their empire; literally, "the parts that in their fourness make up a whole" (Mannheim 1991: 18). The name refers to the four-fold geographic division of the territories that comprised the empire.

tambo [S.][Q. *tampu*]   Waystation along the Inka road, with barracks and storehouses; used by the army and by travelers on official state business.

tupu [Q.]   From *tupuy*, to measure. The reckoning of a *tupu* of land depends upon the state of the land (in production, in fallow), the vertical ecozone in which the land is located, and other, similar environmental factors. In terms of land allocated to a household, the *tupu* measurement was often governed by the requirements (e.g., the size) of the household. A *tupu* is, therefore, a variable measurement.

wanu [Q.]   Guano; excrement of marine birds (e.g., guanay cormorant, Peruvian booby) whose habitat is primarily on the south Peruvian coast and offshore islands. High in potassium, it was used in agriculture as a fertilizer.

waqcha [Q.]   A poor person, in the sense of a person who lacks family ties and, therefore, also lacks claims to reciprocal services or resources.

yanapaq [Q. *yanapaqkuna*, plural]   From *yanapay*, reciprocal services without accounts being kept. A *yanapaq* was a personal retainer of a political authority. The Inka organized groups of *yanapaqkuna* who were required to work in mines or to herd large flocks of state-owned camelids. Under the Spaniards, the term altered to *anacona* or simply *yana*.

Some Terms for Central Andean Ecozones:

along a trajectory from the Pacific coast east to the Amazon rainforest

yunga [Q. *yunka*]   River valleys on the lower western Andean slopes (≈ 500-2,500 masl) that are warmer, sunnier, and more sheltered than lower elevations toward the Pacific coast. Warm weather crops such as maize, coca, and tropical fruits that are not adapted to the cooler coastal zone often thrive in the *yunka*.

lomas [S.]	Arid central Andean ecozone that currently reaches from the Pacific coastal desert to an altitude of approximately 2,000 masl. A zone that once experienced seasonal, dense belts of sea fog that supported plants and attracted wild camelids and deer just inland from the coast. The *lomas* desert continues to rise along the western mountain slopes, manifesting a prevailing eastward trend of aridity.
qiswa [Q.]	A highland ecozone between about 2,000 and 3,800 masl on the western slopes of the Andean mountain chain. Known as the rainfall agriculture zone, the *qiswa* is highly suitable for Andean domesticated staples: tubers (potatoes) and grains (quinua). The *qiswa* lies above the Pacific coastal desert and the desertified *lomas* zone, and below the grasslands of the high, cold *puna*.
puna [Q.]	Located at high altitudes ranging from approximately 3,800 to 5,000 masl and above, the *puna* was devoted to the herding of camelids (domesticated llamas and alpacas) in prehistory. Grasslands and shrublands up to the lower edge of permanent ice and snow sustain camelids. Cold, arid conditions with exaggerated diurnal temperatures facilitate freeze drying of potatoes (ch'uñu) and llama meat (ch'arki).
altiplano [Q.]	A vast, high plateau located between the western and eastern Andean cordilleras, at their widest; (average altitude ≈ 3,650 masl). The *altiplano* reaches from the southern limits of Lake Titicaca, through Bolivia, south to NW Argentina and N. Chile.
ceja de selva [S.]	Literally "the eyebrow of the jungle", the *ceja de selva* ecozone is located on the eastern slopes of the Andes, just above the Amazon rainforest. Beginning at an elevation of about 1,000 masl, this zone continues unevenly up to elevations of 2,000 to 3,000 m. Unlike the predominantly dry conditions that constrain life on the western Andean slopes, the eastern *ceja de selva* is often wet and heavily forested. Coca was an essential crop cultivated in this zone in prehistory.

This glossary was prepared by Heather Lechtman and Frank Salomon. Frank Salomon wrote the introductory note.

Mapa Ecológico del Perú

Joseph A. Tosi, Jr.

Joseph Tosi's *Mapa Ecológico del Perú* consists of three sheets, each of which measures 58 cm x 82 cm. As part of the map legend, he included information about the date, sponsorship, and printing of the map. This information appears on all three sheets.

Preparado y Publicado por el
Instituto Interamericano de Ciencias Agrícolas
de la Organización de los Estados Americanos (OEA)
Zona Andina
Proyecto 39 - Programa de Cooperación Técnica
Lima, Perú - 1957
Proyecto y Dirección: Joseph A. Tosi Jr., Ecólogo
Impreso en los Talleres del Instituto Geográfico Militar 1958

Sheet 1: the North Sector, sheet 2: the Center Sector, and sheet 3: the South Sector, when assembled, cover the geographic area of present day Peru. Figure 1 in this volume, a highly reduced assembly of the three sheets, presents the major ecological zones to which Murra refers.

Tosi completed the map in 1957; it was printed in 1958. In his first lecture, Murra remarks that the map was published by the Agrarian University in Peru. It is likely that he acquired a copy of the map at that institution. The map was not formally published and made available until 1960 (see Lecture 1, Footnote 2).

We scanned each of the original sheets, edited them to ensure color fidelity and uniformity, and reduced each sheet in order to incorporate them here, at the end of this volume.

Heather Lechtman

John V. Murra Bibliography

Murra, John V. 1946. "The Historic Tribes of Ecuador." In *Handbook of South American Indians*, Vol. 2, *The Andean Civilizations*, edited by Julian H. Steward, 785-821. Washington, D.C.: Smithsonian Institution, Bureau of American Ethnology, Bulletin 143.

———. 1956. "The Economic Organization of the Inca State." PhD diss., University of Chicago.

———. 1962a. "Cloth and its Functions in the Inca State." *American Anthropologist* 64(4): 710-728.

———. 1962b. "An Archaeological 'Restudy' of an Andean Ethnohistorical Account." *American Antiquity* 28: 1-4.

———. 1964. "Una Apreciación Etnológica de la Visita." In *Visita Hecha a la Provincia de Chucuito por Garci Diez de San Miguel en el Año 1567*, compiled by John V. Murra, 421-444. Lima: Casa de la Cultura del Perú.

———. 1965. "Herds and Herders in the Inca State." In *Man, Culture, and Animals*, edited by Anthony Leeds and Andrew P. Vayda, 185-215. Washington, D.C.: American Association for the Advancement of Science.

———. 1967. "La Visita de los Chupachu como Fuente Etnológico." In *Visita de la Provincia de León de Huánuco en 1562*, edited by John V. Murra, t. 1, 383-417. Huánuco: Universidad Nacional Hermilio Valdizán.

———. 1968a. "An Aymara Kingdom in 1567." *Ethnohistory* 15: 115-151.

———. 1968b. "La Papa, el Maíz, y los Ritos del Tawantinsuyu." *AMARU, Revista de Artes y Ciencias de la Universidad Nacional de Ingeniería*, Lima (octubre): 58-61.

———. 1972. "El 'Control Vertical' de Un Máximo de Pisos Ecológicos en la Economía de las Sociedades Andinas." In *Visita de la Provincia de León de Huánuco en 1562*, edited by John V. Murra, t. 2, 429-476. Huánuco: Universidad Nacional Hermilio Valdizán. [Republished in JVM, *Formaciones*].

———. 1975a. *Formaciones Económicas y Políticas del Mundo Andino*. Lima: Instituto de Estudios Peruanos.

———. 1975b. "Las Etno-categorías de Un *Khipu* Estatal." In *Homenaje a Gonzalo Aguirre Beltrán*, edited by Roberto Bravo Garcón, Vol. 2, 167-176. México: Universidad de Veracruzana y Instituto Indigenista Interamericano, 1974. [Republished in JVM, *Formaciones*].

————. 1980a [1956]. *The Economic Organization of the Inka State*. Greenwich: JAI Press.

————. 1980b. "From Corvée to Retainership." In Murra, *The Economic Organization of the Inka State*, 153-186. Greenwich: JAI Press.

————. 1980c. "Peasant Corvée and the Revenues of the State." In Murra, *The Economic Organization of the Inka State*, 89-119. Greenwhich: JAI Press.

————. 1980d. "The Disposal of Surplus or the Redistributive State." In Murra, *The Economic Organization of the Inka State*, 121-137. Greenwich: JAI Press.

————. 1981. "The 'Vertical Control' of A Maximum of Ecologic Tiers in the Economies of Andean Societies," translated from the Spanish by D. Chavin Escobar and Gabriel Escobar M. [This manuscript is unpublished. It is located in the JV Murra Papers, Series VIII, Box 2 of the National Anthropological Archives, Smithsonian Institution, Washington, D.C.]

————. 1985a. "El 'Archipiélago Vertical' Revisited." In *Andean Ecology and Civilization*, edited by Shozo Masuda, Izumi Shimada, and Craig Morris, 3-13. Tokyo: University of Tokyo Press.

————. 1985b. "The Limits and Limitations of the "Vertical Archipelago" in the Andes." In *Andean Ecology and Civilization*, edited by Shozo Masuda, Izumi Shimada, and Craig Morris, 15-20. Tokyo: University of Tokyo Press.

————. 2002. *El Mundo Andino. Población, Medio Ambiente y Economía*. Lima: Instituto de Estudios Peruanos and Fondo Editorial, Pontificia Universidad Católica del Perú.

Murra, John V., Nathan Wachtel, and Jacques Revel, eds. 1986. *Anthropological History of Andean Polities*. Cambridge: Cambridge University Press, 1986.

Reference List

Adams, Robert McC. 1966. *The Evolution of Urban Society: Early Mesopotamia and Prehispanic Mexico.* Chicago: Aldine.

Alva, Walter and Christopher B. Donnan. 1993. *Royal Tombs of Sipán.* Los Angeles: Fowler Museum of Cultural History.

Arnold, Denise Y. and Elvira Espejo. 2010. *Ciencia de las Mujeres: Experiencias en la Cadena Textil desde los Ayllus de Challapata.* La Paz: Instituto de Lengua y Cultura Aymara.

Baudin, Louis. 1928. *L'Empire Socialiste des Inka.* Paris: Institut d'Ethnologie.

Bennett, Wendell Clark. 1946. "Archaeology of the Central Andes." In *Handbook of South American Indians*, Vol. 2, *The Andean Civilizations*, edited by Julian H. Steward, 61-147. Washington, D.C.: Smithsonian Institution, Bureau of American Ethnology, Bulletin 143.

———. 1953. *Excavations at Wari, Ayacucho, Peru.* New Haven: Yale University Publications in Anthropology No. 49.

———. 1954. *Ancient Arts of the Andes.* New York: Museum of Modern Art.

Bohannon, Paul J. and George Dalton, editors. 1962. *Markets in Africa.* Evanston: Northwestern University Press.

Bourget, Steve and Kimberly L. Jones, eds. 2008. *The Art and Archaeology of the Moche.* Austin: University of Texas Press.

Camino, Alejandro, Jorge Recharte, and Pedro Bidegaray. 1981. "Flexibilidad Calendárica en la Agricultura Tradicional de las Vertientes Orientales de los Andes." In *Runakunap Kawsayninkupaq Rurasqankunaqa. La Tecnología en el Mundo Andino*, edited by Heather Lechtman and Ana María Soldi, 169-194. México: Universidad Nacional Autónoma de México.

Castillo B., Luis Jaime, Hélène Bernier, Gregory Lockard, and Julio Rucabado Yong, eds. 2008. *Arqueología Mochica: Nuevos Enfoques.* Lima: Fondo Editorial, Pontificia Universidad Católica del Perú.

Castro, Victoria, Carlos Aldunate, and Jorge Hidalgo, eds. 2000. *Nispa Ninchis, Conversaciones con John Murra.* Lima: Instituto de Estudios Peruanos and New York, Institute of Andean Research.

Choy, Emilio. 1962. "Desarrollo del Pensamiento Especulativo en la Sociedad Esclavista de los Incas." *Actas y Trabajos, Segundo Congreso Nacional de Historia*, t. II: 87-102.

Cieza de León, Pedro de. 1967 [1553]. *El Señorío de los Incas*. Segunda Parte de *La Crónica del Perú*. Lima: Instituto de Estudios Peruanos.

Collier, Donald and John Victor Murra. 1943. *Survey and Excavations in Southern Ecuador*. Chicago: Field Museum of Natural History, Anthropological Series 35, Publication 528.

Conrad, Geoffrey W. 1993. "Domestic Architecture of the Estuquiña Phase: Estuquiña and San Antonio." In *Domestic Architecture, Ethnicity, and Complementarity in the South-Central Andes*, edited by Mark. S. Aldenderfer, 55-65. Iowa City: University of Iowa Press.

Davis, Emma Lou. 1965. "Small Pressures and Cultural Drift as Explanations for Abandonment of the San Juan Area, New Mexico and Arizona." *American Antiquity* 30: 353-355.

Denevan, William M. 1987. "Abandono de Terrazas en el Perú Andino: Extensión, Causas y Propuestas de Restauración." In *Andenes y Camellones en el Perú Andino*, edited by C.

De la Torre and M. Burga, 255-259. Lima: Consejo Nacional de Ciencias y Tecnología [CONCYTEC].

———. 1995. "Prehistoric Agricultural Methods as Models for Sustainability." *Advances in Plant Pathology* 11: 21-43.

Dewan, Leslie and Dorothy Hosler. 2008. "Ancient Maritime Trade on Balsa Rafts: An Engineering Analysis." *Journal of Anthropological Research* 64: 19-40.

Diez de San Miguel, Garci. 1964. *Visita Hecha a la Provincia de Chucuito por Garci Diez de San Miguel en el Año 1567*, compiled by John V. Murra. Lima: Ediciones de la Casa de la Cultura del Perú.

Donnan, Christopher B.1978. *Moche Art of Peru*. Los Angeles: Museum of Cultural History, University of California.

Engels, Friedrich. 1902 [1884]. *The Origin of the Family, Private Property and the State: In the Light of the Researches of Lewis H. Morgan*, translated by Ernest Untermann. Chicago: Charles H. Kerr.

Estete, Miguel de. (1918) [1535]. "Noticia del Perú." *Boletín de la Sociedad Ecuatoriana de Estudios Históricos Americanos*, Quito 1(3).

Finley, Moses. 1954. *The World of Odysseus*. New York: Viking Press.

———. 1973. *The Ancient Economy*. Berkeley: University of California Press.

Flannery, Kent. V. 1964. "The Middle Formative of the Tehuacan Valley: Its Pattern and Place in Mesoamerican Prehistory." PhD diss., University of Chicago.

———. 1967. "The Vertebrate Fauna and Hunting Patterns." In *The Prehistory of the Tehuacan Valley*, Vol. 1, *Environment and Subsistence*, edited by Douglas S. Byers, 132-177. Austin: University of Texas Press.

Flannery, Kent V., Joyce Marcus, and Robert G. Reynolds. 1989. *The Flocks of the Wamani: A Study of Llama Herders on the Punas of Ayacucho, Peru*. San Diego: Academic Press.

Flores O., Jorge A. and Juan Núñez del Prado B., eds. 1983. *Q'ero. El Último Ayllu Inka: Homenaje a Óscar Núñez del Prado Castro*. Qosqo: Centro de Estudios Andinos Cuzco.

Flores O., Jorge A., Juan Núñez del Prado B. and Manuel Castillo F., eds. 2005. *Q'ero, el Último Ayllu Inka. Homenaje a Óscar Núñez del Prado y a la Expedición Científica de la UNSAAC* [Universidad Nacional de San Antonio Abad del Cusco] *a la Nación Q'ero en 1955*. Lima: Fondo Editorial de la Universidad Nacional Mayor de San Marcos, and Instituto Nacional de Cultura, Cusco.

Fonseca Martel, César. 1972a. "Sistemas Económicos en las Comunidades Campesinas del Perú." PhD diss., Universidad Nacional Mayor de San Marcos.

———. 1972b. "La Economía "Vertical" y la Economía de Mercado en las Comunidades Alteñas del Perú." In Ortiz. *Visita de la Provincia de León de Huánuco en 1562*, t. 2, edited by John V. Murra, 315-338. Huánuco: Universidad Nacional Hermilio Valdizán.

Garcilaso de la Vega, Inca. 1991[1609]. *Comentarios Reales de los Incas,* Vol. 1, edited by Carlos Araníbar, 345. México DF: Fondo de Cultura Económico.

Garnsey, Peter, Keith Hopkins, and C.R. Whittaker, eds. 1983. *Trade in the Ancient Economy.* Berkeley and Los Angeles: University of California Press.

Gato, Guillermo. "Declaraciones de Don Guillermo Gato." In *Visita y Composición que el Marqués de Valdelirios, Juez y Visitador General de Tierras, Hizo en Términos y Juridicción de la Ciudad del Cuzco, 1711-1714.* Lima: Archivo Nacional, Títulos de Propiedad, cuaderno 454.

Godelier, Maurice. 1975 [1964]. "La Noción de Modo de Producción Asiático y los Esquemas Marxistas de Evolución de las Sociedades." In Maurice Godelier, Karl Marx et al. *Sobre el Modo de Producción Asiático,* translated by Alberto Méndez, 13-64. Barcelona: Ediciones Martínez Roca.

———. 1987 [1969]. *Las Sociedades Primitivas y el Nacimiento de las Sociedades de Clases Según Marx y Engels: Un Balance Crítico,* translated by Mario Arrubla and Jorge Orlando Melo. Bogotá: La Oveja Negra.

Goldstein, Paul S. 2000. "Communities Without Borders: The Vertical Archipelago and Diaspora Communities in the Southern Andes." In *The Archaeology of Communities,* edited by Marcello A. Canuto and Jason Yaeger, 182-209. London: Routledge.

———. 2013. "Embedded Andean Economic Systems and the Expansive Tiwanaku State: A Case for a State Without Market Exchange." In *Merchants, Markets, and Exchange in the Pre-Columbian World,* edited by Kenneth G. Hirth and Joanne Pillsbury, 361-387. Washington, D.C.: Dumbarton Oaks Research Library and Collection.

Guaman Poma de Ayala, Felipe. 1936 [1613]. *Nueva Corónica y Buen Gobierno.* Paris: Institut d'Ethnologie.

———. 1980 [1615]. *Nueva Corónica y Buen Gobierno,* edited by John V. Murra and Rolena Adorno; traducciones quechuas by Jorge L. Urioste. México: Siglo XXI.

Gyarmati, János and András Varga. 1999. *The Chacaras of War. An Inka State Estate in the Cochabamba Valley, Bolivia.* Budapest: Museum of Ethnography.

Hagen, Victor W. von. 1964. *The Desert Kingdoms of Peru.* London: Weidenfeld and Nicolson.

Hartmann, Roswith. 1968. "Maerkte im Alten Peru." PhD diss., Universitaet zu Bonn.

Healy, Kevin. 2001. *Llamas, Weavings, and Organic Chocolate: Multicultural Grassroots Development in the Andes and Amazon of Bolivia.* Notre Dame: University of Notre Dame Press.

Helmer, Marie. 1955-1956. "La Visitación de los Yndios Chupachos: Inka et Encomendero." *Travaux de l'Institut Française d'Études Andines* 5: 3-50.

Hyslop, John. 1984. *The Inka Road System.* New York: Academic Press.

Knudson, Kelly J. 2008. "Tiwanaku Influence in the South Central Andes: Strontium Isotope Analysis and Middle Horizon Migration." *Latin American Antiquity* 19: 3-23.

Knudson, Kelly J., Paul S. Goldstein, Allisen Dahlstedt, Andrew Somerville, and Margaret J. Schoeninger. 2014. "Paleomobility in the Tiwanaku Diaspora: Biogeochemical Analyses at Rio Muerto, Moquegua, Peru." *American Journal of Physical Anthropology* 155 (3): 405-421.

Kosok, Paul. 1965. *Life, Land and Water in Ancient Peru.* New York: Long Island University Press.

Kroeber, Alfred. 1944. *Peruvian Archaeology in 1942.* New York: The Viking Fund Publications in Anthropology No. 4.

La Barre, Weston. 1948. *The Aymara Indians of the Lake Titicaca Plateau, Bolivia.* American Anthropologist Memoir No. 68.

Lanning, Edward P. 1967. *Peru Before the Incas.* Englewood Cliffs: Prentice-Hall.

Lechtman, Heather. 1993. "Technologies of Power: The Andean Case." In *Configurations of Power: Holistic Anthropology in Theory and Practice*, edited by John S. Henderson and Patricia J. Netherly, 244-280. Ithaca: Cornell University Press.

Lumbreras, Luis, G. 1974. *The Peoples and Cultures of Ancient Peru.* Trans. Betty J. Meggers. Washington, D.C.: Smithsonian Institution Press.

McCown, Theodore D. 1945. "Pre-Incaic Huamachuco: Survey and Excavations in the Northern Sierra of Peru." *University of California Publications in American Archaeology and Ethnology* 39 (4): 223-399.

MacNeish, Richard S. 1967. "An Interdisciplinary Approach to an Archaeological Problem." In *The Prehistory of the Tehuacan Valley*, Vol. 1, *Environment and Subsistence*, edited by Douglas S. Byers, 14-24. Austin: University of Texas Press.

———. 1970. "Megafauna and Man from Ayacucho, Highland Peru." *Science* 168: 975-978.

Mamani, Mauricio. 1981. "El Chuño: Preparación, Uso, Almacenamiento." In *Runakunap Kawsayninkupaq Rurasqankunaqa. La Tecnología en el Mundo Andino*, edited by Heather Lechtman and Ana María Soldi, 235-246. México: Universidad Nacional Autónoma de México.

Mannhein, Bruce. 1991. *The Language of the Inka since the European Invasion*. Austin: University of Texas Press.

Maquet, Jacques J. 1961. *The Premise of Inequality in Rwanda*. London: Oxford University Press.

Mayer, Enrique and César Fonseca Martel. 1979. *Sistemas Agrarios en la Cuenca del Río Cañete, Departamento de Lima*. Lima: Oficina Nacional de Evaluación de Recursos Naturales [ONERN].

Morgan, Arthur E. 1946. *Nowhere Was Somewhere: How History Makes Utopias and Utopias Make History*. Durham: University of North Carolina Press.

Morgan, Lewis Henry. 1851. *The League of the Ho-de-no-sau-nee or Iroquois*. Rochester: Sage and Brothers.

———. 1877. *Ancient Society: or, Researches in the Lines of Human Progress from Savagery, Through Barbarism to Civilization*. New York: H. Holt and Company.

Morris, Craig. 1967. "Storage in Tawantinsuyu." PhD diss., University of Chicago.

———. 1982. "The Infrastructure of Inka Control in the Peruvian Central Highlands." In *The Inca and Aztec States 1400-1800*, edited by George A. Collier, Renato I. Rosaldo, and John Wirth, 153-171. New York: Academic Press.

———. 1986. "Storage, Supply, and Redistribution in the Economy of the Inka State." In *Anthropological History of Andean Polities*, edited by John V, Murra, Nathan Wachtel, and Jacques Revel, 59-68. Cambridge: Cambridge University Press.

———. 1992a. "Huánuco Pampa and Tunsukancha: Major and Minor Nodes in the Inka Storage Network." In *Inka Storage Systems*, edited by Terry Y. Levine, 151-175. Norman: University of Oklahoma Press.

———. 1992b. "The Technology of Highland Inka Food Storage." In *Inka Storage Systems*, edited by Terry Y. Levine, 237-258. Norman: University of Oklahoma Press.

———. 1993. "The Wealth of a Native American State: Value, Investment, and Mobilization in the Inka Economy." In *Configurations of Power*, edited by John. S. Henderson and Patricia J. Netherly, 36-50. Ithaca: Cornell University Press.

Moseley, Michael E. and Kent C. Day, eds. 1982. *Chan Chan: Andean Desert City*. Albuquerque: University of New Mexico Press.

Munn, Nancy D. 1986. *The Fame of Gawa: A Symbolic Study of Value Transformation in a Massim (Papua New Guinea) Society*. Cambridge: Cambridge University Press.

Netherly, Patricia Joan. 1978. *Local Level Lords on the North Coast of Peru*. Ann Arbor: University Microfilms International..

Ortiz de Zúñiga, Iñigo. 1972. *Visita de la Provincia de León de Huánuco en 1562*, edited by John V. Murra. Huánuco: Universidad Nacional Hermilio Valdizán. Tomo 1, *Visita de las Cuatro Waranqa de los Chupachu*, 1967. Tomo 2, *Visita de los Yacha y Mitmaqkuna Cuzqueños Encomendados en Juan Sanchez Falcon*.

Palerm, Ángel. 1957. *Studies in Human Ecology*. Washington, D.C.: Anthropological Society of Washington, Pan American Union.

Pillsbury, Joanne, ed. 2001. *Moche Art and Archaeology in Ancient Peru*. Washington, D.C.: National Gallery of Art.

Polanyi, Karl, Conrad M. Arensberg, and Harry W. Pearson. 1957. *Trade and Markets in the Early Empires*. Glencoe: The Free Press.

Polo de Andegardo, Juan. 1940 [1561]. "Informe al Licenciado Briviesca de Muñatones [...]." *Revista Histórica (Lima)* t.13: 125-196.

Prescott, William H. 1847. *History of the Conquest of Peru*. Philadelphia: Lippincott.

Pulgar Vidal, Javier. 1946. *Los Ocho Regiones Naturales del Perú*. Lima: Universidad Nacional Mayor de San Marcos.

Quilter, Jeffrey and Luis Jaime Castillo B., eds. 2010. *New Perspectives on Moche Political Organization*. Washington, D.C.: Dumbarton Oaks Research Library and Collection.

Rice, Don S. 1993. "Late Intermediate Period Domestic Architecture and Residential Organization at La Yaral." In *Domestic Architecture, Ethnicity, and Complementarity in the South-Central Andes*, edited by Mark S. Aldenderfer, 66-82. Iowa City: University of Iowa Press.

Rostworowski de Diez Canseco, María. 1964. "Nuevos Aportes para el Estudio de la Medición de Tierras en el Virreinato e Incario." *Revista del Archivo Nacional del Perú* 28/I-II: 31-58.

———. 1970. "Mercaderes del Valle de Chincha en la Época Prehispánica: Un Documento y Unos Comentarios." *Revista Española de Antropología Americana* 5: 135-177.

———. 1978. *Señoríos Indígenas de Lima y Canta*. Lima: Instituto de Estudios Peruanos.

———. 2005. "Sucesiones, Correinado e Incesto Real entre los Incas." In Rostworoski, *Ensayos de Historia Andina* I, 27-35. Lima: Instituto de Estudios Peruanos.

Rowe, Ann Pollard, ed. 1986. *The Junius B. Bird Conference on Andean Textiles*. Washington, D.C.: The Textile Museum.

Rowe, Ann Pollard, Elizabeth P. Benson, and Anne-Louise Schaffer, eds. 1979. *The Junius B. Bird Pre-Columbian Textile Conference*. Washington, D.C.: The Textile Museum and Dumbarton Oaks.

Rowe, John Howland. 1946. "Inca Culture at the Time of the Spanish Conquest." In *Handbook of South American Indians*, Vol. 2, *The Andean Civilizations*, edited by Julian H. Steward, 183-330. New York: Cooper Square Publishers.

———. 1962. "Stages and Periods in Archaeological Interpretation." *Southwestern Journal of Anthropology* 18(1): 40-54.

———. 1984. "An Interview with John V. Murra." *Hispanic American Historical Review* 64 (1984): 633-653.

Sahlins, Marshall. 1972. *Stone Age Economies*. Chicago: Aldine-Atherton.

Salcamaygua, Joan de Santa Cruz Pachacuti Yamqui. 1968 [1613]. "Relación de Antigüedades Deste Reyno del Perú." In *Crónicas Peruanas de Interés Indígena* t. 209, edited by Francisco Esteve Barba, 279-319. Madrid: Biblioteca de Autores Españoles.

Sámano-Xerez, Francisco de. 1937 [1534]. "Relación." In *Cuadernos de Historia del Perú*, edited by R. Porras Barrenechea, 63-68. Paris: Imprimerie Les Presses Modernes t. 2.

Sanders, William T. 1970. *The Natural Environment, Contemporary Occupation and 16th Century Population of the Teotihuacan Valley*. University Park: Pennsylvania State University.

Santillana, Julián Idilio. 1999. "Andenes, Canales y Paisaje." In *Los Incas: Arte y Símbolos*, edited by Franklin Pease, 61-108. Lima: Banco de Crédito del Perú.

Shimada, Izumi. 1995. *Cultura Sicán. Dios, Riqueza y Poder en la Costa Norte del Perú*. Lima: Edubanco Continental.

Silverblatt, Irene. 1987. *Moon, Sun, and Witches*. Princeton: Princeton University Press.

Stanish, Charles. 1989. "Household Archeology: Testing Models of Zonal Complementarity in the South Central Andes." *American Anthropologist* 91: 7-24.

Steward, Julian H. 1955. *Irrigation Civilizations*. Washington, D.C.: Pan American Union.

Strathern, Marilyn. 1992. *After Nature: English Kinship in the Late Twentieth Century*. Cambridge: Cambridge University Press.

Strong, William Duncan. 1957. *Paracas, Nazca, and Tiahuanacoid Relationships in South Coastal Peru*. Salt Lake City: Society for American Archaeology, Memoir 13.

Stumer, Louis M. 1958. "Contactos Foráneos en la Arquitectura de la Costa Central." *Revista del Museo Nacional (Lima)* 27: 11-30.

Sutter, Richard. C. 2000. "Prehistoric Genetic and Culture Change: A Bioarchaeological Search for Pre-Inka Altiplano Colonies in the Coastal Valleys of Moquegua, Peru, and Azapa, Chile." *Latin American Antiquity* 11: 43-70.

Tello, Julio C. 1930. "Andean Civilization. Some Problems of Peruvian Archaeology." In *The Life and Writings of Julio C. Tello*, edited by Richard L. Burger, 279-316. Iowa City: University of Iowa Press, 2009 [1930]. This article was republished from Tello. "Andean Civilizations." *Papers of the 23rd International Congress of Americanists*, New York: 259-290.

———. 1942. "Origen y Desarrollo de las Civilizaciones Prehistóricas Andinas." *Actas del XXVII Congreso Internacional de Americanistas*, Lima: 589-720.

Thomas, R. Brooke. 1979. "Effects of Change on High Mountain Human Adaptive Patterns." In *High Altitude Geoecology*, edited by Patrick J. Webber, 139-188. Boulder: Westview Press.

Tosi, Jr., Joseph A. 1958. *Mapa Ecológico del Perú*. Lima: Instituto Interamericano de Ciencias Agrícolas de la OEA, Zona Andina.

Tosi, Jr., Joseph A. and L.R. Holdridge. 1960. *Zonas de Vida Natural en el Perú: Memoria Explicativa sobre el Mapa Ecológico del Perú*. Turrialba (Costa Rica): Instituto Interamericano de Ciencias Agrícolas de la OEA, Zona Andina. *Boletín Técnico No. 5*.

Treacy, John M. 1994. *Las Chacras de Coporaque: Andenería y Riego en el Valle del Colca*. Lima: Instituto de Estudios Peruanos.

Treacy, John M. and William M. Denevan.1994. "The Creation of Cultivable Land through Terracing." In *The Archaeology of Garden and Field*, edited by Naomi F. Miller and Kathryn L. Gleason, 91-110. Philadelphia: University of Pennsylvania Press.

Turner, Victor. 1969. *The Ritual Process: Structure and Anti-structure*. Chicago: Aldine.

Uceda C., Santiago and Elías Mujica B., eds. 1994. *Moche: Propuestas y Perspectivas*. Trujillo: Universidad de la Libertad.

Ugent, Donald. 1970. "The Potato." *Science* 170: 1161-1166.

Urton, Gary. 2014. "From Middle Horizon Cord-Keeping to the Rise of Inka Khipus in the Central Andes." *Antiquity* 88: 205-221.

———. 2017. *Inka History in Knots.* Austin: University of Texas Press.

Valencia Zegarra, Alfredo. 2004. "Recent Archaeological Investigations at Machu Picchu." In *Machu Picchu*, edited by Richard L. Burger and Lucy C. Salazar, 71-82. New Haven: Yale University Press.

Vinicio Rueda, Marco and Segundo Moreno Yánez, eds. 1995. *Cosmos, Hombre y Sacralidad.* Quito: Abya Yala.

Wachtel, Nathan. 1982. "The *Mitimas* of the Cochabamba Valley: the Colonization Policy of Huayna Capac." In *The Inca and Aztec States 1400-1800*, edited by George A. Collier, Renato I. Rosaldo, and John D. Wirth, 199-235. New York: Academic Press.

Wedin, Åke. 1963. *La Cronología de la Historia Incaica.* Gotemburgo: Instituto Ibero-Americano.

White, Leslie A., ed. 1940. *Pioneers in American Anthropology: the Bandelier-Morgan Letters, 1873-1883.* Albuquerque: University of New Mexico Press.

Wittfogel, Karl A. 1957. *Oriental Despotism: A Comparative Study of Total Power.* New Haven: Yale University Press.

Wolf, Eric R. 1981. "Ángel Palerm Vich 1917-1980." *American Anthropologist* 83: 612-615.

Wolf de Romero, Freda Yancy. 1996. "An Interview with John Victor Murra." *Lima Times*, August: 31-32.

Index

HAU Books is committed to publishing the most distinguished texts in classic and advanced anthropological theory. The titles aim to situate ethnography as the prime heuristic of anthropology, and return it to the forefront of conceptual developments in the discipline. HAU Books is sponsored by some of the world's most distinguished anthropology departments and research institutions, and releases its titles in both print editions and open-access formats.

www.haubooks.com